DIVING

WITH

SHARKS

and other
Adventure Dives

DIVING
WITH
SHARKS

and other
Adventure Dives

Jack Jackson

PASSPORT BOOKS
NTC/Contemporary Publishing Group

PASSPORT BOOKS
NTC/Contemporary Publishing Group

This edition first published in 2001
by Passport Books, a division of
NTC /Contemporary Publishing Group Inc.
4255 West Touhy Avenue
Lincolnwood (Chicago), Illinois 60712-1975
U.S.A.

ISBN 0-658-01459-5

Library of Congress Catalog Card Number: 00-135383
Published in conjunction with New Holland Publishers (UK) Ltd

PUBLISHER Mariëlle Renssen
MANAGING EDITORS Claudia dos Santos (SA),
Mari Roberts (UK)
MANAGING ART EDITOR Peter Bosman
EDITOR Gill Gordon
PICTURE RESEARCHER Sonya Meyer
ILLUSTRATORS Steven Felmore, Anton Krugel
PRODUCTION Myrna Collins

Reproduction by
Hirt & Carter (Pty) Ltd, Cape Town
Printed and bound in Singapore by
Tien Wah Press (Pte) Ltd

2 4 6 8 10 9 7 5 3 1

HALF TITLE *Suspended between ancient columns, Grand Cenote.*
TITLE *A steel mesh-clad diver offers a meal to a small shark at
one of the many dedicated shark feeding dives in the Bahamas.*
RIGHT *Most qualified divers enjoy exploring wrecks in shallow
to mid-depth waters, but penetration and exploration of deep
wrecks requires specialized skills and training - Shinkoku
Maru, Truk Lagoon, Micronesia.*

CONTENTS

RIGHT *Although they are the biggest fish in the sea, whale sharks feed on plankton and pose no real danger to divers or snorkellers.*
FOLLOWING PAGE *Manta Rays' enlarged pectoral fins give the appearance of flapping wings as they fly effortlessly through the water.*

INTRODUCTION

IVING IS AN ADVENTUROUS SPORT, although what actually constitutes an adventure will vary with each individual's psyche and diving proficiency. For recently qualified divers, the adventure is diving itself, but once their dive log begins to fill up and they have enough experience to operate their equipment without thinking, most divers will crave fresh adventures.

For many divers, interaction with marine animals is the greatest thrill. On land, even on the great plains of Africa, one is lucky to get within binocular distance of wild animals. Underwater, on the other hand, one regularly gets within arm's length and has to resist the temptation to touch. Sharks, most of which are harmless, strike fear into most people, but there are divers who love them and will do anything to see the larger ones in their natural environment. Diving amongst predatory sharks, or even just viewing them from the safety of a cage, involves suppressing one's fear and, if one is honest, this is a principal part of the adventure. Whale or Basking Sharks may be gentle giants, but swimming with them is an occasion when the adrenaline rush is not about fleeing, but concerns chasing to keep the animal in sight. Close encounters with other large marine animals, such as Giant Groupers, dolphins, stingrays, Manta Rays and turtles, will thrill even the most experienced of divers; while sea snakes are more deadly than their counterparts on land. The underwater world offers up a wealth of animal and plant species, many of which are only studied by scientists, but divers soon come to know and recognize many of the species they regularly encounter.

Gentle drift-dives are an effortless way of viewing the scenery, but high-voltage drift-dives in strong currents produce adrenaline rush after adrenaline rush as divers are swept uncontrollably towards walls, boulders or coral heads, then just when they are sure that they will collide with them, they are swept to one side.

Swimming around a wreck or penetrating open, well-lit gangways requires only the minimum level of training; whereas cavern diving, despite the diver always being in sight of daylight, and lengthways penetration of wrecks, require training that will enable divers to take the correct action if something goes wrong. Divers who are constantly seeking new challenges will continue to push the limits; diving under ice, penetrating deeps wrecks, exploring caves or aiming for depth records.

In the 1950s, pioneering underwater photographers, Hans and Lotte Hass, enthralled television viewers with films of their adventures. In those early days they used oxygen rebreathers: divers breathed oxygen, their exhaled gases were chemically cleaned of carbon dioxide, more oxygen was added and the gases rebreathed. In 1941 Hass got together with Hermann Stelzner, the technical director of equipment manufacturer Dräger in Germany and together they converted the Dräger-Gegenlunge rebreather to make it more suitable for swimming; divers could now swim freely underwater with fewer noisy bubbles to scare the fish away. A disadvantage was that oxygen has a shallow depth limit. Divers sometimes forgot this and accidents occurred.

Jacques-Yves Cousteau, the French diver and early explorer, also experimented with oxygen rebreathers but suffered oxygen convulsions. He tried using compressed air with an apparatus developed by Yves le Prieu and Maurice Fernez, but was not happy with it. He later asked demand valve engineer Émile Gagnan if he could produce a demand valve suitable for diving. Gagnan's first attempt gave too much air when Cousteau swam head-up, and too little when he swam head-down. This problem was solved by positioning the valve as close as possible to the level of the diver's lungs and, in June 1943, Gagnan delivered a new design: the aqualung, albeit a twin-hose version, was born.

In the early days, scuba diving was only practiced by a few dedicated explorers who had no specialized training, and used only basic equipment, but as society became more affluent and people enjoyed more leisure time, dive training agencies blossomed worldwide. Recreational diving has today become a multimillion-dollar industry with certification agencies, dive operators, travel destinations and equipment manufacturers all competing for their share of the lucrative market.

Basic certification is only the beginning. It gives divers a credit card-sized C-card that enables them to get scuba cylinders filled with air and to dive with any diving operator. Most warm-water divers prefer a minimalist approach, using a single scuba cylinder and regulator. Apart from monitoring depth, time and air supply, they are free to concentrate on the beauty of their surroundings. However, more experienced divers, and those diving in cold water, particularly under ice or when penetrating deep wrecks or caves, soon realized the need for redundancy (carrying completely separate spare items of equipment to allow for malfunctions). Cave divers operating at large distances from the exit must be self-reliant on air or gas supplies, lights and guide lines for navigating back to the surface. Pioneering cave divers, who had to carry large amounts of equipment for deep diving and making long decompression stops, initially adopted the equipment and techniques used by commercial and military divers, until they later evolved their own.

In order to reduce the problems associated with nitrogen and oxygen at depth, divers use gas mixtures other than normal air, which enable them to dive further and for longer. This is termed 'extended range' or 'technical' diving. Nitrox (air enriched with oxygen), enables longer dive times and shortens decompression times but can only be used at shallow depths. Trimix (where helium replaces some of the oxygen and nitrogen), allows deeper diving but the breathing mixes have to be altered as the diver descends and ascends. Diving in this way using open-circuit scuba equipment requires many separate cylinders of different breathing mixes, each with its own regulator; and this has led to the development of rebreathers, which allow the gas mixture to be modified as the depth of the dive varies.

So recreational diving has come full circle. It began with oxygen rebreathers, changed to open-circuit scuba on air and is now returning to rebreathers, albeit using different gas mixtures. Ever adventurous, divers have taken up the challenge, and embraced the freedom that modern rebreather design makes feasible – and who knows what will be possible in the future.

It must be noted that many of the dives in this book are not suitable for novices. On some dives, the diver needs to be completely self-sufficient and have enough experience to take the correct remedial action for safety, without having to think, if things go wrong. Deep diving and all diving in enclosed overhead environments requires special training in the discipline concerned. It is of paramount importance that divers complete the necessary training before commencing such dives.

OPPOSITE *Close encounters with sharks and other marine species are the objective of many dives, but regardless of whether the encounters are deliberate (top) or inadvertent (bottom), divers must remember to behave at all times in an environmentally responsible manner.*

TOP *Modern rebreathers exemplify the latest in technological innovation and allow suitably qualified divers to dive deeper and stay longer underwater.*

ABOVE *Caverns and caves can be dark and frightening, or reveal a world of unexpected beauty and wonder, but being closed environments, they are dangerous and require the highest levels of diving skill and training.*

PROTECTING THE DIVER'S ENVIRONMENT

The sea, particularly its coral reefs, is a great 'theme park' for divers, a colourful undersea world which drives thriving tourist industries – some of which support the economies of entire nations. These huge limestone reefs have been built by tiny coral animals over the millennia, but when the living coral polyps are blasted, buried, crushed, overheated, poisoned or smothered, the reefs die.

Unfortunately coral reefs, turtles, sharks and most fish reserves are in trouble today. As a result of modern fishing methods, most edible fish are being over fished to a point where they are being caught faster than they can reproduce – and many other animals are killed incidentally, as by-catch. This is bad enough with species that become sexually mature at an early age and spawn millions of eggs at a time, but sharks, dolphins and turtles do not reach sexual maturity until they are much older, and then produce relatively few offspring – so they are in danger of becoming extinct.

On coral reefs, both blast fishing and cyanide fishing kills indiscriminately. Sewage and agricultural runoff that is rich in nutrients can cause algae to bloom, blotting out the sunlight and oxygen that most animals require to live. Industrial pollution threatens all marine life, while sediment from logging, coral quarrying or construction work smothers the corals, and in recent years, coral bleaching has been a serious problem in some areas.

Divers can be part of the problem. Clumsy, or just ignorant, they may kill live corals with their hands, fins or boat anchors, or make use of boats or resorts that have poor environmental standards. However, it *is* possible to dive environmentally.

Try not to touch living marine organisms with either your body or your diving equipment. Do not wear gloves except on wrecks and keep your equipment tucked away close to your body. Never stand on corals. If you are about to collide with the reef, steady yourself with your fingertips on a part of the reef that is already dead or covered in algae. If you need to adjust your diving equipment or mask, try to do so in a sandy area away from the reef. Control your fins. Their size and the force of kicking can damage large areas of coral. Don't use deep fin-strokes next to the reef or sand, as the surge of water can damage delicate organisms and disturbed sand can smother them.

Be properly weighted, and learn good buoyancy control. If you haven't dived for a while, practise your skills somewhere that you won't cause any damage.

Don't collect or buy shells, corals, starfish or any other marine souvenirs.

On any dive excursion, whether with an operator or privately organized; a one-day outing or a longer trip, all garbage should be collected for proper disposal on land. Avoid using boats that drag anchors over the reef, have bad oil leaks or discharge untreated sewage near reefs. Where fixed moorings exist, make sure that your boat uses them.

Take care in underwater caverns and caves. Keep diver numbers down and don't stay in one place for too long, as air bubbles collecting in pockets below the roof can kill delicate creatures living there.

Don't spear fish, don't move marine organisms around to photograph them and don't hitch rides on turtles or Manta Rays, as it causes them considerable stress.

OPPOSITE *Diving responsibly means ensuring that neither one's body nor any items of equipment come into contact with the reef, as well as respecting the space and habitat preferences of the species one encounters.*
LEFT *Underwater caves and caverns often have fragile ecosystems that are vulnerable to the presence of too many divers.*

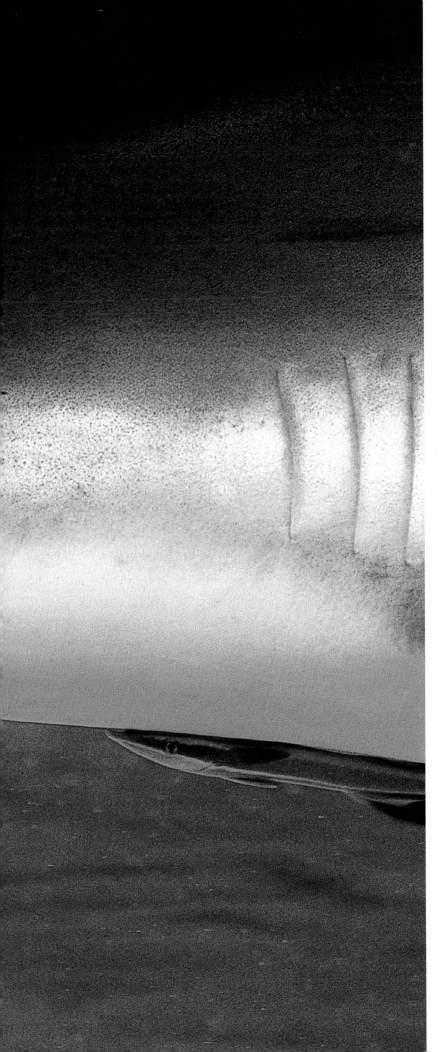

DIVING
WITH
SHARKS

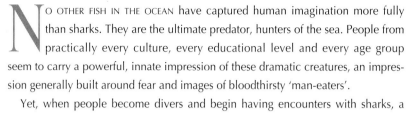

NO OTHER FISH IN THE OCEAN have captured human imagination more fully than sharks. They are the ultimate predator, hunters of the sea. People from practically every culture, every educational level and every age group seem to carry a powerful, innate impression of these dramatic creatures, an impression generally built around fear and images of bloodthirsty 'man-eaters'.

Yet, when people become divers and begin having encounters with sharks, a remarkable change in these impressions takes place. Sharks begin to be perceived as graceful, beautifully formed and supremely adapted creatures. They are seen for their many differences: some species, like Horned Sharks, are tiny, spending their lives hidden on the bottom; others, like the Whale Sharks, are immense plankton feeders with huge bodies, but have a timid, gentle nature that belies their awesome size. Even the more ferocious predatory species, the sharks of movies and night-mares, are discovered to be generally shy around divers, not the eat-everything-in-their-path monsters of imagination. Beyond all, they come to be recognized as animals that are not in some way intrinsically evil, but animals that deserve their place in the natural environment, especially those sharks that serve as apex preda-tors, culling the weak and the sick from marine life populations.

Sharks are among the most fascinating creatures in existence. Like their cousins the rays, their skeletons are made of cartilage, not bone like other fish, and their abrasive skin is covered with tiny versions of their teeth. Predatory sharks also have prodigious sensory powers, such as being able to locate prey, using their ability to sense electromagnetic emissions from other animals' bodies; their sense of smell is so keen that the scent of food can be detected from a consid-erable distance. They also have excellent vision, being able to discern colours and patterns; and they show a surprising level of memory retention – sharks that are fed in a particular location will return to the spot, at the same time, day after day, often swimming for many kilometres for the chance of a free meal.

However, sharks also have a surprising disadvantage, a characteristic that now puts them at risk in the modern world. While most fish breed young and produce thousands, sometimes millions, of eggs at a time, sharks typically don't become sexually mature until they are several years old. Some of the larger species, such as Bull Sharks, may not breed until they are 18–20 years old. When sharks do breed, they engage in individual intercourse and only produce a few young at a time. These may be born alive, or born from eggs either carried inside the mother's body, or laid to hatch. In many parts of the world, where sharks are fished mercilessly, this means their numbers are rapidly dwindling.

Divers may be the first people to truly develop affection for these majestic, mis-understood animals. With cameras in hand, many divers rely on feeding to entice sharks close enough for photography and close observation; this surprises most people, who don't realize that sharks are generally either too shy, or too disinter-ested, to approach people. The shark dives of the world – thrilling and, strangely, emotionally moving – are now diving's hottest ticket. They transform the divers who experience them and change their initial misconceptions and fear to feelings of admiration: awe, respect and a deep regard for one of nature's true wonders.

DIVING
WITH
SHARKS

PREVIOUS PAGES *Sharks such as this Caribbean Reef Shark, seen here accompanied by a Remora, exert a fascination that compels divers to seek close encounters with them in the open sea or from the safety of cages.*

OPPOSITE *Predatory sharks may look fearsome, but most species will not harm scuba divers or snorkellers provided they observe basic precautions.*

TOP *A Scalloped Hammerhead Shark cruises past overhead in the open water.*

ABOVE *At Gansbaai, in the Western Cape, divers can experience Great White Sharks at close range from the security of a sturdy cage.*

RIGHT *Horned Sharks, such as this Port Jackson Shark, are harmless.*

CAGE DIVING WITH SHARKS

Sharks gained their fearsome reputation from observation under unnatural conditions. Ships in anchorages where rubbish was regularly thrown overboard, and wartime battles at sea accompanied by sinking ships, exploding munitions and hundreds of mutilated bodies bleeding profusely in the water caused sharks to gather at the surface to scavenge.

Nowadays we realize that only a few sharks are dangerous to man, although some normally docile sharks may become dangerous to divers if they feel threatened or if there are large amounts of blood and food in the water.

To get close to dangerous sharks, divers use metal cages and then attract the sharks with bait. Great White Sharks, the largest of the predatory sharks, can be found all over the world in coastal temperate waters, even in the Mediterranean Sea, but three areas have become famous for larger concentrations of this species, which gather to feed around seal and sea lion colonies, especially at pupping time. For many years divers concentrated on South Australia, California's southeast Farallon Island, which is restricted for research, and the south and southwest coasts of the Western Cape in South Africa, where the largest populations occur. All these destinations attract increasing numbers of divers.

Another form of cage diving takes place above deep blue-water well out to sea off southern California. The target species here are the less dangerous Blue Sharks, although the bait set out to attract them often also attracts the more dangerous Mako Sharks, relatives of Great White Sharks.

Blue and Mako Sharks – Southern California

Shark diving off southern California is somewhat different from shark diving in other parts of the world because it takes place in blue water well offshore. A cage, constructed of aluminium bars, is lowered from the back of a boat, and suspended from large floats 3–4m (10–13ft) below the surface. This serves as a safe refuge from which to view the sharks, or a frame of reference for divers who wish to view the action from a closer vantage point outside the cage.

Most of the dives are conducted out of San Diego or the Los Angeles–Long Beach areas. Out of San Diego, divers are transported over a broad area some 40km (25 miles) offshore, in open ocean. In the LA–Long Beach area, dives are also in open ocean, chiefly between the mainland and Catalina Island, which lies some 42km (27 miles) offshore. Here, the favourite sites are Avalon Banks and 15-Mile Bank. Boats will also travel even further to the south, to remote San Clemente Island, located nearly 82km (51 miles) from the mainland.

Regardless of the location, Californian shark dives are all conducted in a similar manner. On reaching the chosen area, the boat captain will cut the engines and begin to drift. The next chore is to attract the sharks by putting fish-scraps (called chum) into the water, creating a scent trail that sharks will follow back to the boat. The most commonly used chum is frozen mackerel, an oily fish that creates a lot of scent when it is dispersed in the water. There are a number of methods of preparing chum to create the most effective chum-trail. Some operators chop the fish into small pieces and hang it in gunny sacks (sacks made of coarse material) from the side of the boat, while others place larger chunks of fish in plastic boxes that will let the juices escape. Some also pour their own 'secret' mixtures of animal blood (purchased from meat processors) and ground up fish into the water.

One clever operator out of Los Angeles created the most ingenious approach – a kitchen sink garbage disposal unit, mounted on the boat's live-bait well. Mackerels are ground up in the disposal unit to form a thick puree that spills out of the stern of the boat and drifts away in the current.

Once the chumming has begun, divers prepare their kit and wait for the sharks to show up. Given sharks' amazing sense of smell – they are able to smell prey from a considerable distance away – it usually only takes 45 minutes to an hour before several sharks, chiefly Californian Blue Sharks and the occasional Shortfin Mako Shark, begin to arrive. Once they are close, the crew begins feeding them larger pieces of fish to keep them interested in the boat as the source of the food.

The cage is then lowered into the water and the divers follow, either entering the cage through the top to watch the cruising sharks, or swimming freely among them. The Blue Sharks, slender, sinuous creatures most often around 2m (6.5ft) in length, are generally curious, but nonthreatening. Lovely animals, their skins glow with a cobalt patina that is iridescent in the sunlight. With long, pointed snouts, their mouths are located rather far back under the tip of the nose. When they feed, it is a deliberate motion, with their nictitating membrane (a thin fold of skin beneath the eyelid) coming down to protectively cover the eyes, followed by a slight roll of the body as the food is taken.

On such dives, a moment may come when the Blue Sharks suddenly disappear. Knowledgeable divers begin to look around, as this usually means a Shortfin Mako is about to arrive on the scene. Since Mako Sharks feed on Blue Sharks, the Blues

OPPOSITE TOP *On their way to the cage dive site, dive boat operators prepare chum (ground up fish matter) which is used to attract sharks.*

OPPOSITE BELOW *Strong metal cages are used to protect divers. Once at the site, the cages are lowered into the water and the divers enter them when the sharks are sighted.*

ABOVE *A dive boat operator scans the seas for any sign of activity, such as a shadow or dorsal fin breaking the surface that would indicate the presence of sharks.*

ABOVE *The cobalt-blue colour, long pointed snout and large eyes make the Blue Shark easily identifiable.*
OPPOSITE LEFT TO RIGHT *The set-back jaw line and snaggle-toothed appearance of a Mako Shark; a playful California Sea Lion investigates a diver's fins; a Blue Shark swims through scuba exhaust bubbles.*

give them wide berth. For divers, such moments provide an extra thrill. Mako Sharks are swift, active predators, the fastest sharks in the sea. Much like cheetahs on land, they are able to capture the fastest swimming prey, including tuna, as well as other sharks. The Mako Sharks seen are usually relatively small ones, in the 2m (6.5ft) range. They are generally nervous around divers, their snaggle-toothed expressions appearing fierce as they swim rapidly through the water. However, they don't usually stay around for long and, within moments of their leaving, the Blue Sharks return.

Other open-ocean creatures are also often seen. Opportunistic and intelligent, California Sea Lions seem to taunt the sharks, nipping at their fins and stealing the food. The sea lions are so much more quick and agile than the sharks that they seem to feel no threat from being in their presence, despite being a natural prey of both Blue and Mako sharks. Occasionally divers may also see 'Mola molas', big ungainly Ocean Sunfish with baggy elephant-like skin and large eyes, floating lazily near the surface.

MEMORIES OF A MAJESTIC MAKO

As we dropped into the water the boat drifted off, leaving us alone. An open ocean, blue-water dive is interesting for its quiet peacefulness, drifting suspended in a sea that stretches out of sight in all directions. Visibility was marginal, about 8–10m (25–33ft), and the sun was low, creating a dim, still scene. As we hung weightless in the water, a movement caught my eye. A Sea Lion, graceful, blondish-brown in the dark water, twirled and pirouetted past us. Then another shape moved into view. Dark, huge. I thought – a Great White! The shark had a crescent-shaped tail and was at least 4m (13ft) long; around its belly it was as big as a horse. It passed, then came by again, closer. As it neared, its blue-cast skin and long, snaggly teeth became clear. This wasn't a White; it was a gigantic, female Shortfin Mako.

MAKO SHARK

For the next 25 minutes she studied us intently. The feeling of being under scrutiny from those black, featureless eyes is hard to describe. I realized it was one of those moments when you were caught between real fear and the sure knowledge that you were experiencing something truly rare that may never happen again – a moment I would not have missed for anything in the world.

BLUE SHARK

She circled closer, coming close on several occasions. The skin around her face was scratched and scarred. At one point, she came slowly at us, forcing my dive buddy and I to move apart to avoid being brushed by her massive pectoral fins. At another point, she came straight toward me, overfilling my camera viewfinder; when I looked up, she turned abruptly and passed, my photo just a blurred view as she went by. Back on the boat, we were at first speechless. Then grins replaced the overwhelming sense of wonder at what we had just experienced – some incredible moments shared with true majesty in the sea.

Al Hornsby - PADI Course Director; Group Publisher and Editor: Skin Diver Magazine, Los Angeles.

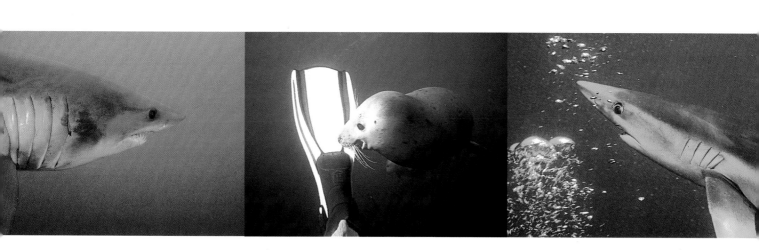

Great White Sharks, Western Cape, South Africa

Great Whites have long been hated and persecuted, but a new breed of eco-adventurer is fast realizing that this incredible predator is more than a simple killing machine; it is a great creation of nature. In 1991 South Africa became the first country to protect the Great White Shark and today, many people make a living from taking tourists, film crews and researchers to see this threatened species.

South Africa is thought to harbour the largest population of Great White Sharks in the world, with the highest concentrations occurring on the south and southwest coasts of the Western Cape, South Africa. The water here is usually between 13 and 19°C (55 and 66°F), creating the perfect temperate water conditions that this shark prefers. The Great Whites spotted off the Cape typically measure around 3.5m (11.5ft), but every year a few intrepid adventurers may get to see the huge 5.5m-plus (18ft) females that are the reproductive future of the species. For cage dives, the sharks are attracted using the chumming method.

There are three prime viewing and dive sites in the Western Cape where, during the winter and early spring months (April through October), cage divers have an exceptionally good chance of seeing Great Whites, as they congregate in these locations each year to breed.

The first is Seal Island in False Bay, on the east coast of the Cape Peninsula, just a few kilometres from Cape Town. The sharks are attracted to its colony of 64,000 Cape Fur Seals and the abundant birdlife, while the surrounding mountain ranges create a scenic site for divers. The area was first opened for scientific study, and to a limited number of regular operators, in 1995. It is unsurpassed for the observation of natural shark behaviour such as predation, due largely to the strict controls exercised over operators. Winter's offshore winds clean and flatten the bay, and average visibility is around 8–10m (26–33ft), reaching 15m-plus (50ft) on good days. Great Whites can be expected in varying numbers on a daily basis. False Bay is home to a legendary shark, called the Submarine, estimated to be 7m-plus (23ft), and the more recently spotted 6m-plus (20ft) creature nicknamed Hercules.

The second site is Dyer Island, off Gansbaai, on the Cape's south coast. This is the best-known site, due to the large number of operators working there (the first operators started up in 1991, with a major influx in 1996). Most of the diving takes place in a channel known as Shark Alley, with Dyer Island on the one side and Geyser Rock, supporting a seal colony, on the seaward side. The shark-viewing season here is slightly longer, from March through November, and even in the

Opposite top *Large numbers of Great White Sharks are found close inshore off the Cape Peninsula and the south coast of the Western Cape.*

Opposite centre *A dive boat takes divers to Shark Alley, between Dyer Island and the coastal village of Gansbaai.*

Opposite below *A Cape Fur Seal leaps out of the water in a desperate attempt to evade a hungry Great White Shark.*

Left *The cage is being lowered into the water. At this stage, the diver's adrenaline is pumping and anticipation is running high.*

Top *Shark dive cages in False Bay are suspended at surface level, and many divers prefer to use a snorkel rather than scuba gear. A hood and a warm exposure suit are essential in the Cape's cold waters. The top of the cage is closed over the divers to prevent an unwanted intrusion by a curious Great White Shark.*

summer months, sharks are sighted on a semi-regular basis by many of the charter operators. In this unprotected area, the winter winds whip up large mountainous seas, which first have to be negotiated to get to the site. On calm days, however, Dyer Island is a good dive site with visibility upwards of 10m (33ft) and sometimes 15m-plus (49ft).

A very select group of operators is based in Mossel Bay, 385km (240 miles) east of Cape Town. Cage diving takes place around a small seal colony based in a relatively sheltered bay that allows the running of expeditions on most days. Visibility here ranges from 5–20m (16–66ft), with water temperature the highest of the three sites. This year-round site peaks from April through October, while shark activity varies greatly in summer (November – March), although Great Whites are often spotted here out of season. (Dive operations close for the main summer holiday period in December.)

As divers enter through the door in the top of the steel cage tied alongside the boat, the bleating of the surrounding seal colonies

ABOVE Divers setting off for a winter (May through August) dive at Gansbaai. BELOW Even from the safety of the boat, the first close-up view of a Great White is enthralling. One wonders who is the watcher, and who the watched!

fades once they enter the eerie silence of the Great White's watery world. Waiting for that first glimpse of the untamed master of the ocean, the general feeling is one of excitement tinged with apprehension. Then, unexpectedly, the broad, toothy smile of a shark glides effortlessly up towards the divers from the surrounding abyss, and the perpetual rocking motion of the cage is forgotten while awe holds them spellbound at the grace with which the huge animal moves.

A swipe of the great tail propels a torrent of water forward, almost knocking the divers off their feet in the cold steel cage, while an even larger shark ousts the one they thought was massive. They cannot

help being mesmerized by the visual impact of the creature banking only feet away, displaying its massive black eyes, a broad, razor-edged smile, and a huge, streamlined body: hydrodynamic predatory perfection.

As the shark glides silently away, swallowed up by the dark ocean, divers yearn for another glimpse – maybe even a closer encounter with this animal of myth and legend. Eventually, it is the coldness of the surrounding water that forces them back to the surface and reality.

ABOVE LEFT *Small fish are eager to take a free handout.*
ABOVE *The economic value of keeping Great White Sharks alive is exemplified by this mural. In many disadvantaged communities, ecotourism has the capacity to generate much-needed revenue on an on-going basis.*
BELOW *A view from inside; this curious Great White is captured by the photographer's lens – the dive has met its objectives.*

AN UNINVITED GUEST

It was one of those red letter days in False Bay. Up to five Great White Sharks, ranging from 3–4.5m (10–15ft), were swimming around the cage with visibility up to 15m (49ft). An enormous female caressed the top of the cage with her mouth, gently biting what was to her a foreign object, with no apparent malice. It was rather to satisfy her curiosity. All this was happening mere inches away. I could clearly make out parasites that had attached themselves to the roof of her mouth, and I had an urge to reach out and rid her of these irritations.

I felt the cage jerk as another Great White bumped the cage from the other side. This had been going on for the last half-hour, but suddenly something was different. The single shudder I had become accustomed to was becoming repetitive. I turned around to face the head of a 3.2m (10.5ft) female shark firmly wedged in the open viewing port of the cage. What happened next was inevitable: sharks cannot move backward, so she started to panic. With massive thrusts of her wildly flailing tail she drove her whole body into the cage with me, buckling metal in her efforts to free herself, trapping me with her in the 1.5m (5ft) confines of the cage. My only option appeared to be to try to lift the shark's head toward the opposite side of the cage and get her to break open that end to swim out. Wedging myself under her gills, I lifted her head to the opposite port and wedged it in the gap. It worked at first, but her head slipped and we were back where we started. I repeated the exercise. This time her tail re-entered the water, gained propulsion and she succeeded in buckling the bars at the opposite end. She powered her way through the cage, sending floats and metal in all directions.

The 'fun' wasn't over yet as she became entangled in the rope securing the cage to the boat and started dragging the cage down. At this point my two colleagues on the boat, Rob Lawrence and Craig Ferreira, had the presence of mind to cut the rope and, fortunately for me, the shark freed herself once there was no longer any tension on it. The cage slowly rose to the surface and I was picked up by the boat. When I climbed on board, although my legs were shaking and the adrenaline pumping, I was on cloud nine. I had experienced what so few ever could, and no harm had been done to either party.

Chris Fallows, diver and proprietor of African Shark Eco-Charters, Cape Town, South Africa.

OPPOSITE *A Great White Shark mouths the bars of a cage in False Bay, Cape Town. A small island in the bay is home to a colony of Cape Fur Seals that provide a steady supply of food for a thriving population of Great White Sharks, including some of legendary proportions.*

Great White Sharks, South Australia

In Australia, Great White Sharks have been recorded from southern Queensland to northwestern Australia, but nowadays cage diving takes place in and around Port Lincoln in South Australia. Dangerous Reef, in Spencer Gulf, to the east of the town, and North and South Neptune Islands, which lie to the southeast, just outside of Spencer Gulf, are breeding grounds for New Zealand Fur Seals and Australian Sea Lions, a favourite prey of Great White Sharks.

Great Whites are not always going to turn up promptly on cue. It will sometimes take days of chumming the water before any appear and by this time, the divers' initial excitement may have faded and boredom taken over. But then comes a sudden cry from one of the crew. Shark! It often takes a few seconds to sink in before the adrenaline starts pumping and everyone rushes on deck in the hope that this is the real thing. And there, cruising slowly past the bait, will be your first Great White Shark, its dorsal fin breaking the surface, reminiscent of the movies.

A blur of activity follows as the crew rushes to get the shark cages overboard while divers kit up and collect their cameras. The divers want to be in the cages, in the water – but in being forced to wait for them to be prepared, the adrenaline flows. When the cages are finally ready and rocking in the swell

ENCOUNTERING A GREAT WHITE

Apart from the large size of older animals and their large serrated teeth, the most obvious physical characteristic of Great White Sharks is the conical snout, which has led to the alternate names Blue or White Pointer. The eyes appear black, the pectoral fins are large and the bodies are countershaded – darker grey or bronze on top, so they are hard to recognize from above against the darker depths below, and white underneath, so that they are difficult to discern against the lighter sky when viewed from below. Stealthy predators, they tend to slowly approach surface-prey, such as seals or sea lions, from below and then attack from the bottom. Surfers and swimmers at the surface have been attacked but the shark rarely eats them, so it is thought to be mostly a case of mistaken identity. When divers encounter Great Whites near the sea floor, they will be inspected, but normally left alone unless they are carrying fish.

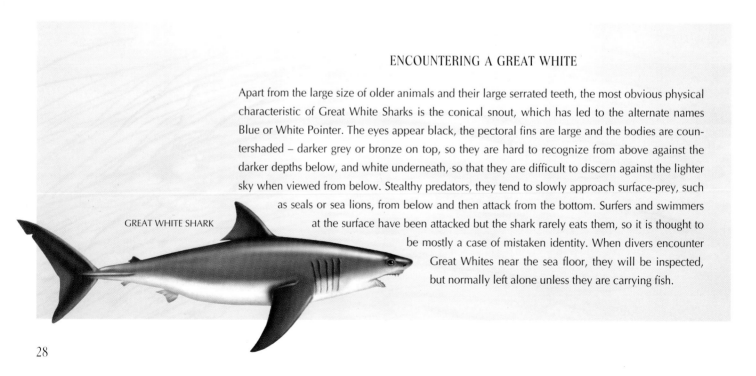

GREAT WHITE SHARK

they seem small and flimsy, up against the large shark, and the doors in their tops appear very exposed. But once given permission to enter, the divers will show no hesitation in jumping into the cages.

Visibility at the surface is often made worse by the chum. A cage could move violently – the result of a shark mouthing the pontoons; it is not trying to get at the divers, rather it is testing the pontoon as it tries to find the source of the chum. Once the divers' senses have acclimatized to the environment, they often realize that there is more than one Great White Shark present. At first the divers are mesmerized by the sharks, but eventually they remember their cameras and set about recording the event. Bracing against the sides of the cages, they point their wide-angle lenses at the action. There is often no time to sight through the viewfinders – especially as they worry about the vulnerability of their hands when they point the cameras through the bars of the cage to avoid having the bars in the picture.

The divers soon run out of film or videotape, but the action is always too awesome to miss, and they tend to remain in the cages until they either run out of air or become too cold. Finally they are forced to climb out and let other divers replace them in the cages. Relaxing in warm clothes and fortified with hot drinks they are tired and happy but, after such an exhilarating experience, the adrenaline is still surging. The experience with Great White Sharks will be the topic of conversation for many hours to come and hopefully the sharks will stay around so that it can be repeated tomorrow.

BELOW This is about as close to a Great White Shark as most divers ever want to get. The rows of razor-sharp teeth are clearly visible. As one falls out, another moves forward to take its place.

One does not have to be an adrenaline junkie to want to cage dive with Great Whites. As the sea's most fearsome predators, they are as attractive to divers as the 'Big Five' mammals are to African safari clients. Experienced divers realize that the image of ruthless killers portrayed in the bait-induced feeding frenzies of sensationalist television documentaries or films such as *Jaws* is far from true.

Enlightened documentary makers are now videoing these sharks using small cameras attached to poles, attached to the sharks (Crittercams) or even hidden in artificial bait, so that they can observe the real behaviour of these animals without having divers in the water.

Diving with Great White Sharks is expensive; they may stay for hours or for only a few minutes; or they may not turn up at all. But there is nothing quite as exciting as a close-up of a Great White Shark from the safety of a cage.

DIVING WITH SHARKS IN THE OPEN SEA

Many shark species cruise the open ocean but the chances of finding them at any given time are minimal. Fortunately, several species are found on shallow continental shelves where there is a plentiful supply of prey. Blacktip Reef, Variegated (Zebra) and Nurse Sharks can be found in shallow water, often inside the reef. Other sharks are found over deep water, feeding on the fish that congregate at nutrient-rich sites. Channels in and out of lagoons carry nutrients on the tide, which feed the fish on which the sharks prey. Fast surface currents, or currents that hit a wall or pinnacle, produce upwellings that carry nutrients from decaying organic matter on the seabed. Where reefs have a pronounced point, currents travelling along either side of the reef at different speeds, mix with the same result.

Some sharks, such as Raggedtooth and Hammerhead Sharks, make migrations, usually following fixed routes with preferred places for mating and pupping. Many sharks prefer the colder water deeper down during the day, rising into shallow water to feed at night, but may be found within sport diving depths during the cooler winter months. Some sharks cruise around seabird colonies at the times when there are unwary chicks in the water, while others hang around ports and estuaries, supplementing their diet by scavenging rubbish.

Taking these factors into account, divers have located several places where shark sightings can be guaranteed when water temperatures are normal, some of which are described in the following pages.

BELOW *Caribbean Reef Sharks congregate at a feed site in the Bahamas.*

The Red Sea

Reefs contain countless colourful sights and a cacophony of sounds as their many inhabitants feed and fight for territory; but in deeper water the colours fade to blue and the sounds to zero. The silence heightens the senses as divers peer into the void, looking for sharks. Timid Whitetip Reef Sharks scurry for the safety of caves and Hammerhead Sharks cruise below in open water, but divers often get a shock as Grey Reef, Silky or Silvertip Sharks suddenly rocket up out of the depths, occasionally harassing the divers out of their territory.

Sha'b Rumi (Roman Reef), a large reef in the Sudanese Red Sea, rises from deep water with its longest sides parallel to the prevailing north–south current. The east side is more contorted than the west, slowing the current down more. When the currents meet again off the narrow south point, they are travelling at different speeds and produce whirlpools and upwellings of nutrients that attract shoals of fish, which in turn, attract large numbers of sharks. In the shelter of the wall, over a sandy plateau descending from 20–36m (65–118ft), up to 50 sharks circle in the early morning: large Silvertips, aggressive, fast swimming Silky Sharks, Grey Reef and Whitetip Reef Sharks while Scalloped Hammerheads shoal over the drop-off.

The reefs called The Brothers, Dædalus, Elphinstone, Rocky Islet, Abington, Sha'b Rumi and Sanganeb have a well-deserved reputation for shark diving but in reality, the common sharks found here can be encountered anywhere, though not

TOP *A harmless Variegated Shark, also known as a Zebra or Leopard Shark in the Red Sea.*

ABOVE *The lighthouse and south jetty at Sanganeb, Sudan.*

TOP *The Brothers islands, in the Egyptian Red Sea, are well-known for rich marine life.*
RIGHT *A group of Grey Reef Sharks (also called Blacktail Sharks) in the Red Sea.*
BELOW *Grey Reef (Blacktail) Shark with remora, off Sanganeb's Southwest Point.*

in such numbers. In general, shark encounters increase as one travels south from Egyptian to Sudanese waters. Whitetip Reef Sharks, Variegated Sharks (also called Leopard or Zebra Sharks), Whitespotted Guitarfish, small Hound Sharks and Nurse Sharks are common everywhere but more likely to be spotted on shallow reefs.

Grey Reef Sharks are curious and therefore seen often on reefs over deep water, in shoals of 5–50, sometimes shoaling with Hammerhead or Silvertip Sharks. Regularly found resting on sand in the early morning, they can be strongly territorial, particularly at dawn and dusk, rushing at a diver and veering off at the last moment.

Silvertips can be among the largest sharks that divers regularly view without cages. The larger ones, heavily-built and accompanied by pilot fish, are quite fearless of divers and will approach within touching distance.

Oceanic Whitetip Sharks mostly stay away from reefs, often shadowing shoals of Pilot Whales, but lone individuals are regularly encountered at The Brothers and Elphinstone. At Dædalus, the normally open water Thresher Sharks are often seen off the northwest and northeast faces.

ABOVE *A diver fends off a troublesome Silky Shark. The easily visible claspers indicate that this shark is a male.*
BELOW *Common along the fringing reefs, Wobbegongs are harmless if not harassed.*

Scalloped Hammerhead Sharks can be found either alone, in shoals of up to 45, or shoaling with Grey Reef Sharks. They prefer depths greater than 70m (230ft) but will rise to check out early morning divers. Elphinstone seems to be the furthest north that divers encounter these sharks in shoals, which get larger and larger as one moves south until the shoals peak at the North Point of Sanganeb. From just north of Elphinstone Reef in Egypt, south to Yemen, timid Blacktip Reef Sharks are rarely seen but they are there, often over the parts of a reef where the water is not deep enough for divers to venture without causing damage to the coral, as, along with Wobbegongs, they are common along fringing reefs. Tiger Sharks are often found around uninhabited islands which act as breeding grounds for seabirds or scavenging garbage off harbours and ships' anchorages.

Pelagic sharks are normally only seen from a boat as divers would not normally dive in open water. Shortfin Mako Sharks, probably the fastest of all sharks, prefer the cooler waters to the north and are often seen in the Gulf of Aqaba, between the Sinai Peninsula and Jordan, while Whale Sharks have been seen everywhere.

ABOVE *Grey Reef Sharks in search of a handout continue to approach divers at Maaya Shark Point, in the Maldives, although formal feeding no longer takes place there.*

The Maldives

The Maldives are a complex collection of 26 separate coral atolls and 1189 different islands and reefs spread across 775km (482 miles) from north to south and for 130km (81 miles) from east to west in the clear, warm Indian Ocean, southwest of the tip of India. The archipelago is one of the world's most exciting and prolific diving areas, with huge expanses of stony and soft corals, throngs of colourful tropical fish and a thriving population of larger marine animals, including Manta Rays, turtles and sharks.

Among the popular dive sites are those occurring around the atolls of North Malé, South Malé, Felidhu, Ari, Vaavu, Vattaru, Rasdhu, Mulaku and Baa. They are reached by dive operations located at the many resorts scattered throughout the Maldives (usually there is only one resort per island). To sample many of the best sites, there are several excellent live-aboard boats that provide 7–14-day safaris, travelling circuits several hundred miles in length.

Due to the government's protective attitude toward the country's marine resources, ocean life is healthy and thriving. A chance cultural attitude helps as well; local islanders seldom eat reef fish, preferring tuna, so this has helped to keep the reef fish population high.

LEFT AND BELOW *The Maldives islands and atolls are built atop one of the largest reef systems in the world. Near-perfect dive conditions, tropical climate and a variety of marine species have contributed to making the country an internationally-popular dive destination.*

There are a number of thrilling shark dives to be enjoyed throughout the Maldives chain, most of them situated at the mouths of channels that cut through the encircling reefs of the atolls. The sharks most often seen in these warm Indian Ocean waters are Grey Reef, Blacktip Reef and Whitetip Reef Sharks, Scalloped Hammerheads and Leopard Sharks.

One excellent shark dive is at a dive site known as Guraidhu Kandu (Guraidhu Corner). As changing tides move large volumes of water in and out of the lagoon, there is a tremendous mix of nutrients at the channel mouth. Clouds of fish gather to feed and these, in turn, attract predators such as sharks, Dogtooth Tuna and large trevallies. Dives at Guraidhu Kandu are best on the incoming flood tide when a brisk current carries divers along the steep coral slope on the outside of the reef, past turtles, shoals of fish, Eagle Rays and many sharks. As the channel opening is reached, the current sweeps inward, carrying delighted divers past coral walls draped with Gorgonian corals and masses of soft corals in brilliant purple, orange and yellow hues.

An especially thrilling dive is at Mulaku Kandu (Mulaku Corner), along the northwest side of Mulaku Atoll, where a channel spills over a 15m-deep (50ft) coral garden at the edge of the reef and a steep wall drops straight down to immeasurable depths. The wall itself is breathtaking; it is covered with rich growths of Gorgonian sea fans, sponges and huge black coral bushes that jut out from the face of the wall. Divers who enter the water at this site just after dawn are often rewarded by a large, milling school of 2–2.5m-long (6–8ft) Scalloped Hammerhead Sharks. These sharks congregate at a depth of around 46m (150ft), their odd, hammer-shaped heads swinging from side to side as they maintain their positions in the gentle current.

The Maldives' best-known shark dive is at Maaya Shark Point, inside the lagoon of Ari Atoll. Here, a long reef rises from a white sand bottom 30m (100ft) deep. The top is a coral garden with reef fish, cuttlefish and many anemones. For many years, large Grey Reef Sharks were hand-fed here and now they show up in large numbers, even when feeding is not occurring. Divers can move along the reef edge as the sharks patrol back and forth, approaching divers to investigate whether food is present; clearly they still associate divers with the availability of a handout. The situation provides an excellent opportunity for shark photography, without the necessity for feeding.

DIVING WITH HAMMERHEAD SHARKS

Cocos and Malpelo Islands, South America

Advanced divers looking for an ultimate thrill without the need to use a shark cage would have to consider swimming with the 'big boys' off Cocos Island. On a good day, the pelagic action here is second to none; the waters teem with Hammerhead, Silky, Silvertip, Grey and Whitetip Reef Sharks; as well as Eagle, Mobula and Manta Rays; and the occasional Whale Shark, a greater density of sharks than anywhere else in the world.

Cocos Island (Isla Del Coco), a small uninhabited, densely wooded volcanic outcrop 480km (300 miles) southwest of the Pacific coast of Costa Rica, is surrounded by volcanic pinnacles up to 0.5km (a quarter-mile) offshore, some of which attract shoals of between 200 and 1000 Hammerhead Sharks.

Normally nocturnal predators, an unusual habit among these Hammerheads is the formation of large, circling shoals during the day, which break up each night to enable the fish to feed singly in deeper waters. The centre of the shoal is normally occupied by the largest, mature females which intimidate the other sharks in the shoal. This is where the males head when they wish to mate. If a female is receptive, she will herd him out of the shoal for a private coupling.

The currents at Cocos Island are strong but the rock is volcanic lava rather than coral, so it is best to hang on to a pinnacle and blend in with it. Breathe as slowly and quietly as possible and the sharks are likely to swim closely past. Most sharks do not seem to be troubled by noise, but Hammerheads are easily freaked by the sound of a diver's exhaust bubbles, so many divers are resorting to Nitrox rebreathers as a way of approaching them more effectively. Divers can usually take a rebreather certification course and also hire rebreathers on the live-aboard dive boats that regularly visit Cocos Island.

STAYING AHEAD OF THE PACK

The most distinguishing physical characteristic of Hammerhead Sharks is their unusually shaped head. Some scientists believe that it helps them with the planing motion, some that by having the eyes farther apart it improves binocular vision, while still others believe the larger area of the head allows them to have an increased number of Ampullae de Lorenzini. Sharks and rays have Ampullae de Lorenzini, sac-like structures linked to small pores in the skin at the front of the head through canals filled with a thick gelatinous substance. Sensitive to mechanical, thermal and salinity stimuli, it is their role as electroreceptors that is most important. These electroreceptors detect the minute electric fields which emanate from animals and metals in sea water, as well as enabling some sharks to detect small variations in the earth's magnetic field for navigation during migration.

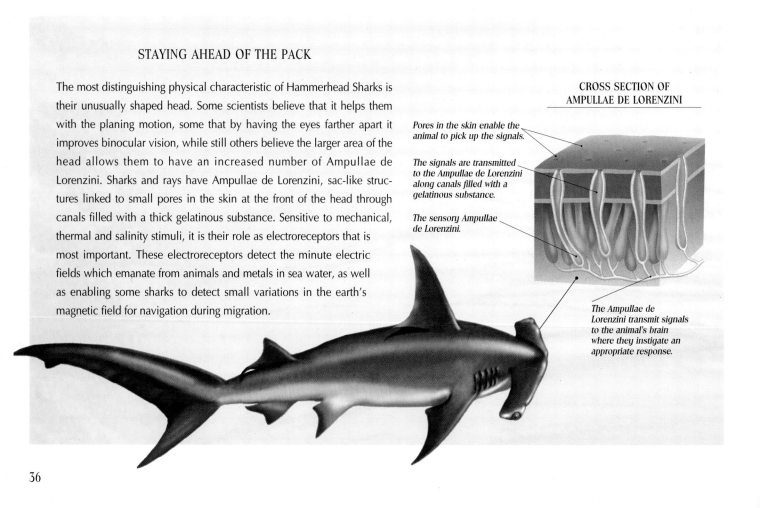

CROSS SECTION OF AMPULLAE DE LORENZINI

Pores in the skin enable the animal to pick up the signals.

The signals are transmitted to the Ampullae de Lorenzini along canals filled with a gelatinous substance.

The sensory Ampullae de Lorenzini.

The Ampullae de Lorenzini transmit signals to the animal's brain where they instigate an appropriate response.

Like most fish, Hammerhead sharks have a preferred water temperature and are usually found in the cooler water below the thermocline (a horizontal, abrupt transition from a warmer to a colder layer of water). During the 1998 El Niño-Southern Oscillation (ENSO) phenomenon, the average water temperatures at 40m (130ft) around Cocos Island rose from 26°C (78°F) to 31°C (87°F), which caused the Hammerhead Sharks to move into deeper water; but they have now returned.

Among the common sights off Cocos Island are shoals of Horse-eye Jacks compressed tightly into balls of fish some 10m (33ft) in diameter as a result of the attention of ever-present predators. Known as 'bait-balls', the shoals are repeatedly attacked by Silky Sharks, Silvertip Sharks, and sometimes Bottlenose Dolphins who crash through the shoal causing a great commotion as they snap up prey. One has to be very careful to remain close to the boat when near to a bait-ball as sharks engrossed in this feeding frenzy have been known to bite a diver's hand by mistake.

At Cocos Island the dives are relatively deep and the currents and surges strong, so most divers surface some distance from the boat cover. All divers should carry a bright orange safety location marker, and a horn or whistle that operates from the compressed air direct feed hose to the BCD.

Malpelo Island, 500km (310 miles) off the western coast of Colombia, is a collection of jagged pinnacles protruding out of the Pacific Ocean where one main pinnacle is larger than the others. Less often visited by divers, the waters here have Scalloped Hammerhead Sharks shoaling at the surface as well as deep below.

A previously unidentified shark has been seen by some divers in this area – although it is similar in appearance to a Grey Nurse (Raggedtooth) Shark, it is reported to be larger and to have bigger eyes. The specimen seen is claimed to be nearly 5m (16ft) long.

ABOVE *Scalloped Hammerhead sharks off the Galapagos Islands.*
BELOW *Whitetip Reef Sharks often congregate on the sand during the day.*

LEFT *This close-up of a Scalloped Hammerhead's snout clearly shows the position of the mouth and the eye.* OPPOSITE TOP *A school of Big-eye Trevallies swirl in the upwellings around the reefs of Terumbu Layang-Layang.* OPPOSITE BELOW *Hammerhead Sharks often shoal in large numbers.*

Hammerhead Sharks, Terumbu Layang-Layang, Malaysia

Almost anywhere in tropical or warm temperate seas where there are strong currents around remote reefs or pinnacles that rise abruptly from deep water, divers can find Hammerhead Sharks. In the past, small groups of these sharks were encountered along walls over deep water, but nowadays, at cooler times of the year, divers are finding large shoals of Hammerhead Sharks either by looking out into the open water or by venturing further away from the reef itself.

Malaysia's Terumbu Layang-Layang is a remote wall-diving site that is famous for large shoals of these majestic creatures rising to depths suitable for experienced sport divers during April and May. The small, barren, low-lying island of covers six hectares (15 acres) on an atoll-like ring of 13 coral reefs linked together. The Malaysian name translates as Swallows Reef but although the western tip of the island has nesting colonies of thousands of Noddy Terns, Sooty Terns, Great Crested Terns and Brown Boobies (sometimes known as Asian Albatrosses), the island does not have any swallows. The early mariners who gave the reef its name did not understand their bird species.

Located 305km (190 miles) northwest of Kota Kinabalu, the capital of Sabah in Borneo, the reefs of Terumbu Layang-Layang rise steeply from a depth of 1830m (6000ft) in the South China Sea. The pristine walls over extremely deep water produce spectacular diving in good visibility. The currents and upwellings attract Manta Rays, turtles, dolphins, big fish and shoals of pelagic and reef species including barracuda, jacks, rainbow runners, tuna, fusiliers, Pennant Butterflyfish, surgeonfish and unicornfish.

Small groups of Hammerhead Sharks can be seen anywhere along the walls. At 'The Valley' they take turns at hanging beside the reef while reef fish clean them of parasites. Whitetip Reef Sharks rest in caves and are so common that they pale into insignificance, while Grey Reef Sharks and Silvertip Sharks are found in deeper water; but it is off the reef's northeast corner that the large shoals of Scalloped Hammerhead Sharks most commonly occur.

Usually found below the thermocline at depths from 45–200m (150–660ft) during the day, shoals of between 45 and several hundred Scalloped Hammerhead Sharks may be seen cruising along parallel to the reef wall, all swimming in the same direction and against the prevailing current. Although normally nocturnal predators, they appear to be using their increased number of Ampullae de Lorenzini (electrical receptors) on their unique hammer-shaped heads by swinging their heads from side to side as if using a metal detector. Sometimes they come very close to the reef while herding shoals of Bigeye Trevallies into shallow water.

Although the area is calm for most of the diving season, the winds can quickly increase in velocity, causing choppy seas and large swells. When these conditions occur, the diving is similar to that off Costa Rica's Cocos Islands, with the same fierce currents, and the more exposed dive sites at Terumbu Layang-Layang are then only suitable for experienced divers.

There are often two thermoclines. Usually the temperature is around 28°C (83°F) at the surface, with a thermocline from 18–24m (60–80ft) where the temperature is around 27°C (80°F). Then from 27m (90ft) down the temperature is 24°C (75°F). It is this deeper, cooler water that the shoals of Scalloped Hammerhead Sharks prefer. As with any area of pelagic action, a lot depends on your luck on the day. The sharks move around, so on one day you might see everything that it is possible to see, and on the next day, absolutely no pelagic species at all while at the same dive site and performing an identical dive profile.

Aliwal Shoal and Protea Banks, KwaZulu-Natal, South Africa

Aliwal Shoal lies 5km (3 miles) off the Green Point lighthouse at Umkomaas, 40km (25 miles) south of Durban, on South Africa's subtropical east coast. Aliwal Shoal was once a sand dune; 80,000 years ago, with the continents shifting and sea levels rising, this was eventually flooded. Shells (calcium carbonate) welded sand particles to make a sandstone core. Today, the shoal has a variety of sponges, some stony and soft corals and, for the serious diver, an amazing biodiversity of flora and fauna. It is accessed in semi-rigid Zodiacs (inflatables) launched from the beach.

Before 1981, Aliwal Shoal was very rarely dived as it had a fearsome reputation for sharks. A local dive operator decided to test it as a viable diving venue in late 1981, and the first boatload of chartered divers, secretly murmuring their last rites in apprehension of what was waiting for them, went out with commercial fishermen. The site has since become one of South Africa's most popular shark-viewing areas, with four dive centres taking divers out to Aliwal Shoal.

TOP *Raggedtooth Shark, Protea Banks.*
BELOW *Anthias swim over the coral encrusted Aliwal Shoal.*

The highlight of this unique and accessible reef is the annual migration of the Spotted Raggedtooth Shark. Adding to often-unforgettable dives are dolphins, turtles, sand sharks, rays, eels, warm- and cold-water reef fish, Humpback Whales on their northern migration, and an annual sardine run.

Raggedtooth Sharks, affectionately known in South Africa as 'raggies', are called Grey Nurse Sharks in Australia and Europe, and Sand Tiger Sharks in the USA. Raggies appear at Aliwal Shoal from the end

of June until the end of November each year, and if dive operators know where the sharks' resting places are, numbers varying between five and 30 individuals will be sighted. Their annual migration focuses on Cape Vidal, which lies within the Greater St Lucia Marine Park, now a World Heritage Site. Here, the spring (September to October) mating jamboree occurs. After mating, the male raggies disappear to an unknown destination – it remains an unresolved question – and the pregnant females head for the warmer waters off Mozambique for a nine-month gestation period. They do not feed during this time, after which they return, aided by the warm south-flowing Agulhas Current, to reach their winter pupping areas off the Eastern Cape, where they can be seen at sites around Port Elizabeth and Plettenberg Bay. The pups are 90cm (3ft) at birth. When they return to Aliwal Shoal, further north, they have grown to 1.2m (4ft). Raggies are sexually mature at seven years, by which time they measure about 1.8m (6ft).

Raggedtooth Sharks are a coastal species and have the unique ability to gulp air and store it in their stomachs for buoyancy control. As a result, raggies can maintain position while facing into a current or surge so that water passes through their gills and enables them to absorb oxygen. Alternatively, the sharks have pre-ferred resting places, in sandy areas, caves, gullies and beneath overhangs, where sufficient water passes through their gills. Aliwal Shoal is one of these areas.

ABOVE *Launching inflatables or Zodiacs (known locally as rubberducks) from the beach is a feature of diving off the subtropical KwaZulu-Natal coast in South Africa.*
BELOW *Raggedtooth Shark – the reason for the name is clearly evident!*

To achieve the best shark diving experience, divers need to have absolute respect for the Raggedtooth's space, that is, they should maintain a distance of 5m (16ft) from its resting area, which is forbidden territory for divers. They also need to breathe slowly and allow exhaled air to trickle out. Sharks are intelligent animals, and if divers attune their movements to the rhythm of the water and the sharks themselves, the raggies will accept the divers as nonthreatening creatures. The Raggedtooth Shark will often close the distance between itself and the divers, allowing them to get up close as it circles to view them or even swims alongside or slowly follows the divers. Sharks tend to be attracted by video cameras. A relaxed Raggedtooth approaching a harmonized group of divers appears not to be affected by a strobe light, although a shark under stress will react to the electromagnetic pulse by disappearing.

It is an incredible diving experience when one is accepted by the raggies and allowed to quietly witness their natural behaviour. If the sharks are left undisturbed at Aliwal Shoal, they will be there for the next group of divers to appreciate.

Protea Banks, another fossilized underwater sand dune, is located 7km (4 miles) offshore between the resort towns of Shelley Beach and Margate, 140km (90 miles) south of Durban. The entire site covers a large area, and its banks, which rise to 27m (90ft), are known as the Northern and Southern Pinnacles.

The first chartered groups of divers started diving at Protea Banks in 1991, using commercial fishing boats to get to the site. Nowadays, if the resident dive charter boat at Umkomaas – the launch site – is booked, there is an alternate permanent charter boat operator (who takes a divemaster and a maximum of eight divers), while another operator is willing to bring his boat from Park Rynie, 20km (12 miles) to the south, for groups of 10 plus a divemaster.

OPPOSITE *A Raggedtooth Shark glides over the reef at Protea Banks.*
ABOVE *Respecting the Raggedtooth's space is the key to a successful dive.*
BELOW *A large Potato Grouper with a juvenile Golden Trevally.*

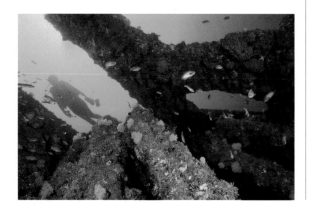

ABOVE *Raggedtooth Sharks are the main attraction of the deep and difficult dives on the pinnacles of Protea Banks.*
BELOW *The coral-encrusted wreck of the Nebo, one of the many ships that has foundered on Aliwal Shoal.*

Launching is through the surf and many operators in this region use RIBs (rigid inflatable boats), known locally as rubberducks. The Northern Pinnacles, which go to a depth of 30–36m (98–118ft) can only be dived when there is no current. Normally, dives are limited to a maximum depth of 30m (98ft). On the Southern Pinnacles, the current carries groups of divers through particular drift lines. The speed is normally one to two knots, but at times reaches four knots. Dive groups go down and come up together, so a thorough predive briefing is essential and participating divers must be certified to 30m (98ft).

The dives at Protea Banks are specifically for shark-viewing, and are not typical reef dives. The areas that are selected for divers to drift through attract big-game fish, so there is a good chance of seeing predators in pursuit. The most common sharks seen from July to September (winter and early spring) are adult Raggedtooth species, while Scalloped, Smooth and Great Hammerhead sharks can be spotted all year round. In the summer months, particularly from September to January, and even right up to June, Bull (Zambezi) Sharks visit South Africa's eastern shores. Other species seen in the area are Great White, Tiger, Blacktip Reef, Dusky (Ridgeback Grey), Bronze Whaler (Copper) and Spinner (Long-nosed Grey) Sharks, as well as Whale Sharks. There is an added possibility of spotting Humpback Whales on their northern migration, as well as schools of Bottlenose Dolphins.

DIVING WITH THE BULLS

We had come to Ponta do Ouro, Mozambique, to film sharks. It is a remote place where the number and variety of species is amazing. In our dives, we were constantly surrounded by Bull Sharks (known here as Zambezi Sharks) and Silvertips. A lone Great Hammerhead eyed us briefly on one dive and a resident 5m-long (16ft) Tiger Shark, while evading our sight, kept us watching the fringes of our vision.

On our last afternoon, just before dark, we dropped from the grey rolling surface down into a rapidly darkening gloom. At 40m (130ft) our guide speared a fish and we were quickly joined by two big – more than 3m (10ft) in length – Bull Sharks and a solitary 2.5m-long (8ft) Silvertip. As they circled I was again impressed by how different the Bulls were to the sharks I had seen at most shark feeds. They were massive, nearly a metre across at the snout, with huge mouths, hinged far back toward the gill slits. Unlike most sharks at feeds, which are only concerned about the food, these sharks were intensely interested in us. They would move in close, closer, then too close, needing a sharp smack on the nose with the camera strobe to keep them away. As the action continued to escalate my buddies, Peter and Stefania Lamberti, two of South Africa's best-known wildlife and underwater photographers and filmmakers, kept giving me bemused looks that said: 'Well, are you getting what you asked for?'

At one point, as Peter's movie lights created a dramatic pool of brightness in the near-black water, one of the big Bulls rushed in. My strobe popped as it banged headlong into Peter's housed digital Betacam. The shark turned and rushed again. Wham! The third time was with open jaws; the marvellous footage that resulted was all shark and teeth, with a perfect soundtrack – hard, sharp, enamel scraping across the housing's aluminium surface.

For more than 20 minutes on the bottom, then during our decompression stop, and even as we clambered into our pitching inflatable boat in the last few minutes before total darkness, the awesome sharks pressed us, bolder and more aggressive than any sharks I have ever seen. Our last sight of the Bulls was of their dorsal fins cutting the surface, as if they were looking for us – still curious, still interested, predators to the very end.

Al Hornsby – PADI Course Director; Group Publisher and Editor, Skin Diver *Magazine, Los Angeles.*

TOP *A Bull Shark accompanied by Remoras, Mozambique. Bull Sharks, also called Zambezi Sharks in this region, have a reputation for aggressive behaviour toward divers.*
ABOVE *In the inky depths of the ocean, the Silvertip Sharks' white fin tips clearly stand out.*

TOP *A diver descends with the 'food box' at Stuart's Cove, closely followed by 'posse' of Caribbean reef sharks.*

ABOVE *Stuart's Cove is one of the best-known shark feed sites in the Bahamas, and has been responsible for introducing many divers to sharks and aspects of shark behaviour.*

OPPOSITE *A variety of sharks and other fish gather around the feeder. Although the sharks regularly feed at the designated sites, there is evidence that they do not rely on them and continue to hunt and feed normally.*

FEEDING SHARKS

Shark feeding varies with species, location and operator. Sharks that protect their eyes and rely on their electro-receptors when biting can be fooled by metal objects, so if the bait is near to a cage, chain or boat, they often mouth these by mistake. For less dangerous sharks, many operators use too much bait in an effort to impress clients. When a large amount of food is hung in mid-water, contact between sharks and divers is rare, as the sharks concentrate on the bait. Where sharks are fed by spear or hand, they equate divers with food and can become boisterous, even without bait in the water. Shark-to-diver contact is possible in these cases, so divers should keep their hands close to their bodies and feeders wear steel-mesh suits and gloves. Shark feeds are more controllable with small quantities of bait hidden in the coral. In a strong current, two dead fish will attract up to 50 sharks, usually circling sedately while trying to locate the bait. This can be preferable for photographers.

The Bahamas

The Bahamas are a collection of more than 3000 islands located just off the US coastline, 75km (45 miles) at their closest point from Florida. They are known for white-sand beaches and clear warm, turquoise water, as well as a tranquil splendour, both above and below the ocean's surface. Besides their famous tropical vacation potential, the islands are also noted for their excellent and varied diving, which takes place among uncountable undersea drop-offs and reefs spread over an area some 800km (500 miles) long, running northwest to southeast. This huge area is full of marine life, with large populations of fish, invertebrates and marine mammals, as well as numerous shipwrecks, the result of maritime disasters from colonial times up until the present day.

However, beyond the beauty and tranquillity, as divers from around the world have discovered, there's more – a wild, high-voltage dive offering that has led to the islands being awarded a top American scuba diving magazine's Travel Hall of Fame Award as 'the shark diving capital of the tropical Atlantic'. Perhaps more than any dive destination in the world, the Bahamas have perfected the art of shark diving at a number of distinct locations and with different methods, all of which successfully create some of the most exciting dive opportunities to be found anywhere. The shark diving activity in the Bahamas is so significant that the islands' dive operators were able to encourage their government to pass legislation prohibiting long-line fishing for sharks because their value as a tourist attraction was shown to far exceed their worth as seafood. Without question, shark diving brings more divers to the Bahamas than any other single dive activity.

The chief centres for shark diving are around Nassau, on New Providence Island; off Grand Bahama; and at tiny Walker's Cay. Another less-known area, frequented by live-aboard boats, is at remote Cay Sal Banks near Bimini. Each location approaches the dives in a slightly different manner but all provide divers with the incomparable thrill of diving up close with the ocean's most intriguing predators. The species usually seen are the sharks most common to the region, including Caribbean Reef, Blacktip Reef and Silky Sharks. Occasionally, however, divers are lucky enough to see more unusual species such as Bull, Lemon, Blue and Great Hammerhead Sharks.

ABOVE *A diver enjoys a "hair-raising" experience at one of Grand Bahama's many shark dive sites. Good buoyancy, regular breathing and steady nerves are essential requirements for diving safely with all predatory sharks.*

Out of Nassau, the Bahamas' capital and tourism hub, there are three main dives, known as Shark Wall, Shark Buoy and Shark Feed. Shark Wall is an undersea drop-off where Caribbean Reef and Blacktip Reef Sharks cruise and can be observed as they patrol the edge of the reef. No feeding takes place here, but the sharks gather in sufficient numbers to provide thrilling dives in a lovely natural setting, complete with a rich collection of corals, sponges and colourful tropical reef fish.

Shark Buoy is an open-ocean dive at an offshore shipping buoy that attracts sharks. Divers hang around the buoy, crystal-clear ocean below them, to observe graceful Silky Sharks, Caribbean Reef Sharks and the occasional Blue Shark that congregate there. As at Shark Wall, feeding is unnecessary at this unique site, which combines the unusual experience of blue-water diving with the spine-tingling excitement of being close to wild sharks. The sharks seem oblivious to the divers' presence and there is no apparent sense of threat.

Nassau's most dramatic shark dive is the shark feed performed by Stuart Cove's dive operation. At a calm, shallow site on a nearby reef, divers kneel on the bottom as the feeder, protected by stainless-steel mesh gloves, uses a short, barbless spear to feed chunks of fish to the Caribbean Reef Sharks. The sharks, usually 2–3m (6.5–10ft) in length, are bulky and strong, with smooth grey skins and dark tips to their fins. The water at the site is very clear and excellent for photography, while the sharks remain quite calm, circling until they come in to take a piece of food. The divers find themselves very close to the sharks, which are interested in the food but non aggressive towards the divers. However, excitement is very high, as there is little more thrilling for divers than being surrounded by 10–20 large sharks at the bottom of the sea.

At Grand Bahama, at the northern edge of the Bahamas and home to the resort centres of Freeport and Port Lucaya, there are well-known dives on a wreck called the *Theo,* as well as with dolphins from Sanctuary Bay. Shark dives are provided by two different dive operations, UNEXSO (Underwater Explorers Society), which also operates the dolphin programme, and Xanadu Divers, both of which use nearby sites called Shark Junction and Shark Alley. Both locations offer calm water over a sandy bottom at a depth of around 15m (50ft) and both operations use a similar approach. While divers kneel in a semi-circle, a feeder, dressed in a full stainless-steel mesh suit, hand-feeds a horde of Caribbean Reef and Blacktip Reef Sharks, which come in from all directions. Some of the female Caribbean Reef Sharks weigh 227kg (500 lb). Other fish, such as groupers and snappers, gather, hoping to grab scraps of food dropped by the sharks. On the sand are many small, sharp shark teeth. These are frequently shed during feeding but are quickly replaced from several rows of backup teeth folded behind those in front.

On UNEXSO's dives, the feeder takes one fish at a time from a plastic container and feeds the sharks individually as they crowd around the scent of the bait. There is a lot of activity here, since as many as 15–20 sharks show up on most dives. By moving up and down the line of divers, the feeder can provide each one with the opportunity to be very close to the sharks as they come in. Particularly interesting is the demonstration of the steel suit's protective capability. By placing a fish on his or her arm or leg, the feeder can trick a shark into biting it. The shark's teeth do not penetrate the steel-mesh and the pressure exerted by its jaws is insufficient to cause the feeder any harm. In addition to watching all the high-octane action, visiting divers can get personally involved by taking a special course to become guest feeders themselves, and don the steel suits for an unforgettable experience.

ABOVE *At shark feeds, such as here at Shark Alley off New Providence Island, divers kneel on the seabed and are careful to keep their limbs still and tucked in close to their bodies.*
BELOW *There are many arguments both in favour of and against feeding fish, but it is generally accepted that in some parts of the world, organized feeds have an important role to play in the conservation of sharks and other marine species.*

THE ETHICS OF FEEDING

Some conservationists argue that feeding fish alters feeding behaviour, affects their health, makes them dependent on divers, and could attract more dangerous predators. Others argue that feeding does not alter long-term behaviour. Most wild animals are opportunistic feeders, not averse to carrion, and the amount of food that divers introduce is minimal, so the fish do not become reliant on them. At Stingray City where the rays are fed many times each day, they are still observed feeding naturally, and at shark feeds a few dominant animals take most of the food while most sharks present go without. Perhaps the most important aspect is that the quantity of divers attracted by organized feeding events causes governments to realize that the animals are worth more kept alive on a sustainable basis than wiped out by fishermen.

RIGHT *As many as 20 sharks at a time can be present during the shark feed at UNEXSO, on Grand Bahama.*
BELOW *Feeders wear full-body suits made of steel-mesh but still need to be constantly alert as they handle numerous hungry sharks.*

At Xanadu Divers, the feeders approach the dives in similar fashion, with hand-feeding and wearing complete steel-mesh suits. Their speciality, however, is in producing an odd form of shark behaviour they've named the 'Xanadu trance'. Enticed to come close by an offering of fish, a shark may become motionless and lie cradled in the feeder's arms when stroked softly around the head and face. This state can become so deep that a shark can appear to fall into a sound sleep, remaining perfectly still while the feeder, holding it by the nose and dorsal fin, walks it around the semi-circle of divers, allowing each one to view the majestic creature from just centimetres away.

At Walker's and Cay Sal (an offshore collection of reefs in the western Bahamas), the approach is more passive, with the bait suspended in the water, allowing the sharks to swarm around while divers move in for the best view. One live-aboard boat's method at Cay Sal is simple; a frozen mass of fish is hung from an underwater line, and divers watch as the sharks come in to feed. There are usually 10–15 moderate-sized Caribbean Reef and Blacktip Reef Sharks that swim near the divers as they approach the bait. From comfortable positions on a soft, sandy bottom at 16m (52ft) to the side of a small, submerged seamount, the divers can take pictures and closely study the sharks' actions.

At Walker's Cay, the Bahamas' northernmost island, the approach is similar. Walker's Cay, long known as one of the world's top game fishing locations, sits on the edge of the deep Atlantic. Fishing boats prowl the open ocean each day and come in with catches of marlin, Sailfish, tuna and Wahoo.

ABOVE *Being in the centre of this sort of action, surrounded by sharks in their natural environment, is what draws divers by the hundred to the world's top shark dives and shark feeding sites. The clearer the water, the better the photographic opportunity.*

ABOVE *A diver is almost obscured by Caribbean Reef Sharks at the Shark Arena feeding site off New Providence.*

RIGHT *A group of sharks feasts on a 'chumsicle', a ball of frozen fish that is suspended from a line at Shark Rodeo, at Walker's Cay in the Bahamas.*

FAR RIGHT *A UNEXSO feeder, clad in steel-mesh, awaits the arrival of his next group of 'lunch guests'.*

Using the fishermen's scraps, the dive operator at Walker's Cay takes the fish parts and freezes them in large, metal drums; the end-products are humourously called 'chumsicles'. A chumsicle is then loaded onto a dive boat and taken to a nearby, shallow site known as Shark Rodeo. When the boat reaches the site, it circles the area a few times as a signal to the sharks that it has arrived, then lowers the chumsicle down on a line to suspend it just above the bottom.

By the time the divers reach the sand at a depth of 15m (49ft), there is a crowd of up to 50 Caribbean Reef, Nurse and Blacktip Reef Sharks, as well as an occasional Great Hammerhead Shark, and a throng of groupers and snappers, all thrashing around the bait, tearing off chunks of fish and gulping them down. The divers can move around the suspended food, staying away or moving close, depending upon their individual comfort level.

For photographers, Shark Rodeo offers an ideal opportunity to get close-up, strobe-lit photographs of large sharks. As in other feeds, the sharks pay little attention to the divers but remain intently interested in the food source. It is obvious that there is fierce competition for the food, as several of the normally passive Nurse Sharks are missing tips of fins and tails, apparently from crowding too close to the more aggressive Caribbean Reef and Blacktip Sharks.

French Polynesia

French Polynesia (generally referred to as Tahiti) is considered one of the most beautiful island groups in the world. Located in the southern Pacific Ocean some 3920km (2430 miles) south of Hawaii, the islands are typically rugged volcanic peaks covered by a deep, green mantle of tropical forest, although there are a few flat, coral atolls. The waters that surround them are crystal clear, in shades of cobalt-blue and turquoise.

The diving in Tahitian waters is characterized by large numbers of fish and healthy coral growth. There are also large populations of sharks, Manta Rays and turtles, and calving grounds where majestic Humpback Whales can be seen close-up, caring for their young. For shark diving, the dive operators of French Polynesia are considered among the founders of the genre, and the shark feeds at Moorea, which were among the first to be developed, have over the years introduced thousands of divers to this unique thrill.

ABOVE *Dive operators on French Polynesia, also called Tahiti, were among the pioneers of shark diving and the many islands in the group offer a variety of exciting shark encounters.*
RIGHT AND OPPOSITE *At Moorea, numerous small tropical fish species congregate around the feeder and a diver, often swooping in to snatch pieces of fish from the feeder's hand.*

The most popular shark site off Moorea, a small island just 19km (12 miles) from the capital, Papeete, is a place called Tiki, on the northwestern shore. A stony coral slope extends downward from the reef-line, and sharks are hand-fed pieces of fish by handlers wearing steel-mesh gloves. A huge number of reef fish gather as the feed begins, especially Bluelined Snappers, Rainbow Runners and Black Triggerfish, usually enough to completely hide the feeder among them. When the sharks begin to arrive, often as many as 30–40 Blacktip Reef Sharks at a time, the scene can erupt into a wild show as the sharks cut in and out of the mass of smaller fish, snatching pieces of bait from the feeder's hand. Divers here are regularly treated to sightings of more unusual sharks as well; a 3m-long (10ft) Lemon Shark is a regular visitor, and occasionally, an awesome 5m-long (16ft) Tiger Shark makes a dramatic – and never-to-be forgotten – appearance.

French Polynesia's other exciting dives offer natural encounters with large numbers of sharks where feeding is not necessary – the northeastern part of the island group, the Marquesas chain, features wild, unexplored diving areas full of sharks and other marine creatures.

Around the remote islands of Eiao and Hatutu, divers may not only find themselves surrounded by hundreds of Pygmy Killer Whales, but will also have close-up encounters with large Silvertip Sharks on virtually every dive. Especially around Eiao, which is home to a major rookery for boobies, terns and frigate birds, Silvertips ceaselessly patrol the waters along the bottom of the steep cliffs that line the shore. Besides being closely approached by Silvertip Sharks, divers will have close encounters in these waters with shoals of Scalloped Hammerhead and solitary Great Hammerhead Sharks, some of them big – as much as 3–4m (10–13ft) in length.

The islands' most inspiring shark encounters are those at distant Rangiroa, an atoll 316km (197 miles) northeast of Papeete. The huge, tadpole-shaped lagoon, more than 75km (50 miles) long and 23km (14 miles) wide, has a large channel opening that is the scene of frenetic marine life activity on each turn of the tide. Divers move along the sides of the cut as a parade of Mantas, Eagle Rays and massive schools of fish pass by. Grey Reef, Whitetip Reef and Blacktip Reef Sharks by the tens and twenties swarm in the food-rich water. At certain times of the year huge Whale Sharks, the largest fish in the sea, migrate through the area, giving visiting divers thrills like none other.

BELOW *Although sharks are the main attraction of diving in French Polynesia, other marine species, such as this Spotted Eagle Ray, can be seen.*

DIVING WITH SHARKS IN AQUARIUMS

Although diving in an aquarium is not every person's idea of a good dive, several countries now have marine aquariums that offer this amenity among their displays, and many people will consider this as their only chance to safely approach predatory sharks and other big fish.

Two Oceans Aquarium, Cape Town, South Africa

Cape Town's Two Oceans Aquarium offers a unique opportunity for qualified scuba divers to dive in the its two main exhibits – the I&J Predator Tank and the Kelp Forest.

The large Predator Tank contains two million litres (450,000 gal) of sea water and is home to five Raggedtooth (Sand Tiger) Sharks as well as schooling local fish species such as Yellowtail Amberjack, Garrick (Leervis) and rays. Occasionally a Sunfish (*Mola Mola*) may be added for a temporary display.

As for that guaranteed shark experience – qualified divers are able to have thrilling close encounters with these magnificent animals without the hindrance of a cage, yet under the skilled guidance of an aquarium diver. For most divers, it is impossible to plan, or even predict such spectacularly close encounters in the wild – and certainly not to guarantee it. As one of the aquarium divers points out, just contemplating the Two Oceans Aquarium shark encounter means that 'the adrenaline starts flowing well before you actually enter the water!'

Visiting divers are unfortunately excluded from the regular Sunday treat when the Raggedtooth Sharks are hand-fed, and devour pieces of fish stuffed with vitamins and juicy Pilchards, offered to them on a special fork. At feeding times there always is some risk that their natural predatory instincts may lead to unpredictable behaviour.

For those who prefer their ocean without sharks, there is an equally exciting opportunity to dive in the Kelp Forest exhibit. The Two Oceans' second largest display, containing 800,000 litres (180,000 gal) of water, allows divers to experience the haunting amber beauty of the kelp forests typical of the Cape's cold west coast, diving between schools of local baitfish such as Maasbankers, Red Roman, Red and White Stumpnose, as well as Galjoen, the national fish of South Africa, and a popular angling species; it is a fierce fighter when hooked. Several Pyjama Sharks also grace these swaying, golden forests. For a touch of added excitement, qualified divers may arrange to help feed this multitude of fish and experience the greedy ocean dwellers swarming about them in search of their share.

TOP LEFT *At the Two Oceans Aquarium in Cape Town, divers can swim in a tank that replicates the kelp forests typical of the cold waters of the Cape's west coast.* ABOVE *Only qualified divers may enter the large open-ocean tank when the Raggedtooth Sharks (raggies), are fed.* BELOW *The aquarium contains many of the larger fish species common to the Western Cape.*

Seaquarium, Curaçao, Lesser Antilles

The Seaquarium on Curaçao, in the Caribbean, was one of the first to offer the facility to dive with sharks, building natural tidal pools beside the main aquarium to house Lemon and Nurse Sharks, turtles, Stingrays and reef fish. The sharks are kept behind five big Plexiglas windows, which have 6cm (2in) holes cut out of them through which divers can hand-feed the animals with safety.

After a short briefing, divers are given a container of small sardine-like fish to clip to their BCDs and they then slide into water just a few metres deep. Stingrays immediately accost them, on the lookout for handouts of fish. The suction from their mouths may bruise bare skin but they have had their venomous spines removed so there is no danger. Tarpon, remoras and Sergeant Majors will also compete for the bait but most divers are more interested in feeding the sharks and huge Jewfish on the other side of the Plexiglas screen.

The windows in the screen are hardly noticeable underwater, so with careful lighting the sharks can be photographed and filmed close up as they take the bait. Jewfish, Lemon Sharks and Nurse Sharks can appear to be quite large. At first it is a little disturbing when the divers stuff the bait through the small holes in the screens and the animals approach, but the big fish are well mannered and the divers soon relax and enjoy the experience.

Another tank at Seaquarium contains huge turtles that wrestle each other out of the way in an attempt to gain dominance at the feeding holes. The proprietor of the Seaquarium shop will make a video of the dive on request, which can then be purchased as a record.

Underwater World, Perth, Australia

The oceanarium at Underwater World, just 20 minutes' drive along the coast from Perth in Western Australia offers divers and landlubbers the opportunity to view several species of shark, plus a variety of other marine animals, in a three-million-litre (660,000gal) aquarium. A 98m (322ft) tunnel with a moving walkway runs through and around the tank, allowing all visitors a close encounter with the marine inhabitants – not that it isn't safe for divers in the tank of course.

Nevertheless, for divers, the experience of sitting on the bottom and looking up as a large shark passes a few centimetres above one's head, with another, even larger, moving up behind it, rows of razor-sharp teeth clearly visible, gets the adrenaline pumping more than most people can imagine.

The shark species at Underwater World usually include large Grey Nurse Sharks, small Whalers, Port Jackson Sharks, Wobbegongs and Carpet Sharks. Although they are all relatively harmless, certain precautions must be taken. Divers are accompanied by an oceanarium divemaster, who advises them to keep to the bottom and never to touch or bump the sharks; they may think it's feeding time, or if they get a fright that disrupts their swimming pattern, it may cause the shoals of trevally, bream, and snapper to panic. The safety of the inhabitants is of prime importance!

After the first adrenaline rush with the sharks, most divers focus their attention on the other 70-plus species of marine life in this oceanarium. Turtles, eels, giant groupers, stingarees and enormous black stingrays are huge attention-grabbers, while smaller fish species are often inquisitive of divers and their camera equipment. The potential for great close-up photographs of fish at Underwater World has resulted in the oceanarium establishing organized dives for photography students. There is never a shortage of stunning photographic material and the courses are very popular. For anyone wishing to meet face to face with sharks and other marine life in a safe environment, this oversized aquarium is the place to be.

Top *Divers at Underwater World can experience the thrill of diving with predatory sharks, but are cautioned to keep well away from them at all times.*
Above *A well-constructed aquarium recreates landscapes that are very similar to those encountered in the natural environment.*
Left *The walk-through tunnel enables non divers to have their own underwater encounters.*

DIVING
WITH
GENTLE
GIANTS

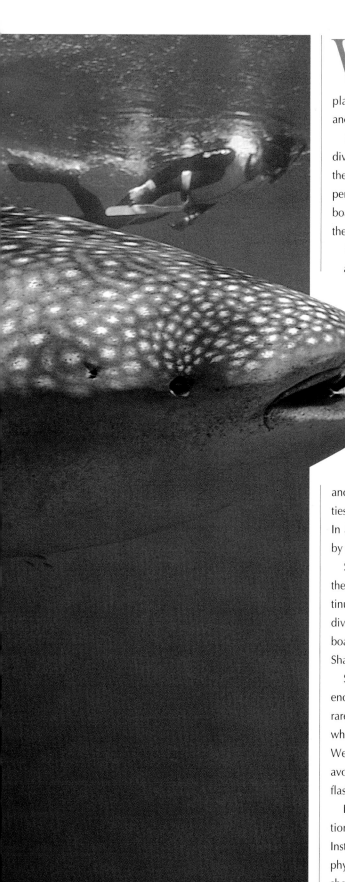

WHALE SHARKS – THE GENTLE GIANTS OF THE SEA – are the largest sharks and the largest cold-blooded animals in the world. They make long migrations in all warm seas except the Mediterranean, following seasonal plankton blooms or upwellings, which attract increased feeding activity by the anchovies, sardines and krill (a shrimplike crustacean) that form much of their diet.

Spotter planes and microlights are often used to guide the boats which carry divers seeking the thrill of swimming with Whale Sharks. The pilots easily pick out the animals and also monitor the divers and report their position to the boat skipper if necessary. Following directions given by the pilot, the skipper will ease the boat ahead of any Whale Shark spotted in the water and, crossing its path, will slip the engines into neutral and give the 'all clear' for divers to quietly enter the water.

It is an indescribable experience when, moments later, a huge broad mouth appears, followed by an awesome body, which can reach 12m (40ft) in length. Whale Sharks are curious creatures, and will often slow down to inspect divers and snorkellers or even stop and 'stand' vertically on their tails. Unable to close their tiny eyes, they draw them in as they approach. The huge slate-grey or grey-brown body is decorated with white spots and bars and covered in parasites. Usually the shark is surrounded by an assortment of fish, including Cobia, juvenile Golden Trevallies and Remoras.

Feeding is an awesome sight. Driven by their immense tails, nearly 1.8m (6ft) high, they cruise through a shoal of krill and anchovies with their huge mouths agape and gills expanded, gulping large quantities of water and sieving the food through spongy tissue between their gill arches. In an adult, the mouth can be nearly 2m (6ft) across and feeding is accompanied by a violent shaking of the head as if to force the food down its throat.

Some Whale Sharks appear to enjoy the presence of divers, particularly when the divers scratch their throats as if they were giant cleaner fish, while others continue on their way, the pressure-wave generated by their movement gently pushing divers and snorkellers aside. Generally, divers surface to be picked up by the dive boat, take a rest and then try again. In this way, where congregations of Whale Sharks occur, they may make 10 or more dives in a day.

Swimming with Whale Sharks used to be considered a once-in-a-lifetime experience – purely a matter of chance – as they were thought to cruise the open sea and rarely be seen at the surface. However, scientists have now located several places where the food supply causes annual gatherings to take place. Ningaloo Reef in Western Australia has become so popular that visitors have to be controlled to avoid harassing the animals. Only snorkelling is allowed and underwater lights or flash guns (strobes) are banned, although scuba equipment is permitted elsewhere.

Little is known about where Whale Sharks come from or go to, but an international research programme is underway. In the Seychelles, the Shark Research Institute is monitoring Whale Sharks, sexing them and using tagging and photography as a means of identification. Large plastic tags are attached to the base of the shark's dorsal fin to enable researchers to follow their movements. Divers also have the option of flying as a spotter-cum-photographer in the microlight aircraft.

DIVING
WITH
GENTLE
GIANTS

PREVIOUS PAGES *The body of a Whale Shark is decorated with white spots and bars.*
OPPOSITE AND TOP *Snorkelling is often the easiest way to keep up with such a power-ful animal, as divers are not restricted by a BCD and scuba cylinder. The speed at which the whale shark swims quickly saps one's energy, and most encounters are over quickly, but good boat cover ensures that the experience can be repeated.*
CENTRE *A diver in Thailand's Andaman Sea stops shooting video to get a clear, close look at a Whale Shark as it swims past .*
RIGHT *Remora hitching a ride on the gills of a Whale Shark.*

ABOVE *A diver looks up from the reef as a Whale Shark swims overhead at Richelieu Rock.*

OPPOSITE TOP *The camera catches a Whale Shark silhouetted against the sun at Richelieu Rock.*

BOTTOM LEFT *Whale Sharks usually swim near to the surface.*

BOTTOM CENTRE *A young Whale Shark catches the diver's eye on a swim past.* BOTTOM RIGHT *Whale Sharks are easy to see from a spotter-plane, Ponta do Ouro, Mozambique.*

Andaman Sea, Thailand

Diving with the biggest fish in the sea is no less of an adrenaline rush than cage diving with Great White Sharks. The ease with which you can approach Whale Sharks makes no difference to this rare encounter, as swimming within touching distance of an animal the size of a small bus is an overwhelming experience that makes the heart rate speed into overdrive.

Camouflaged among Cobia, juvenile Jacks and large Remoras, a lone Whale Shark will often approach divers with an open mouth but when it gets close, closes its mouth and passes between the divers at touching distance, while the pressure wave pushes them aside. At other times the Whale Sharks appear in groups of two or three and may hang around. Often, if the divers just float quietly in the water, these majestic animals will approach them as if they are as interested in the divers as the divers are in them. And one is just as awe-struck when a 5m (18ft) teenager cruises by as one would be if it were a 10m (32ft) adult.

Richelieu Rock, a pinnacle rising from a depth of 33m (108ft) to the surface, 14km (9 miles) east–southeast of Thailand's Surin Island (Koh Surin), is famous for these Whale Shark encounters. This lonely rock, small enough to be circled several times in a single dive, is located in the middle of a large expanse of open sea, and it causes frequent upwellings, which deliver planktonic meals for many species. Huge filter-feeding Whale Sharks often stay in the area for extended periods.

Currents can be strong at Richelieu Rock, but the pinnacle acts as a shelter so there is always a protected side, a welcome place to catch one's breath after chasing the animals in open water. Even if no Whale Sharks show up, there is still plenty to see. By circling the rock in an upward spiral, divers can view an amazing diversity of marine life at every depth, from Requiem and Guitar Sharks to cuttlefish, nudibranchs and Harlequin Shrimps.

Sometimes, while the divers are resting between dives, a Whale Shark will swim around the boat for 10–15 minutes. Slipping quickly into the water with only snorkelling equipment, the divers will find that without the drag of a BCD and scuba cylinder, it is much easier to keep up with the animal as it swims.

Whale Sharks are seen regularly throughout the Andaman Sea, on Thailand's west coast. They appear to migrate northward from the Malaysian border during January and February to reach the border with Myanmar (Burma) during February and March. Another similar area where Whale Shark sightings are almost guaranteed is near the northern end of the Strait of Malacca at Hin Mouang (Purple Rock) and nearby Hin Daeng (Red Rock), 37km (23 miles) south–southwest of Koh Lanta (the names come from the colourful soft corals found on the rocks).

Hin Mouang, a series of submerged pinnacles over a drop-off exceeding 70m (235ft), is the deepest drop-off in Thai waters. Hin Daeng is a series of walls descending in steps to 35m (115ft). As with Richelieu Rock, these isolated pinnacles cause nutrient-rich upwellings that attract a variety of pelagic species. A 4m-long (13ft) young Whale Shark has been seen here so regularly that local dive operators have nicknamed him Oscar.

Ningaloo Reef, Western Australia

The Ningaloo Reef Marine Park, one of Australia's most important tracts of reef, is unique because of its proximity to the coast and its marine life. It supports over 250 species of corals, about 600 species of molluscs, and more than 500 species of fish. It is also the most reliable area in the world where Whale Sharks can be observed and studied.

Ningaloo Reef runs parallel to the Cape Range Peninsula in Western Australia. It extends for approximately 260km (160 miles) and the outer reef runs from between 7km (4 miles) to less than 200m (220 yd) offshore. The different ecosystems within these boundaries support variety of marine life. Dugong (sea cows whose forelimbs have adapted to form flippers) feed on sea-grasses in the shallow lagoons, turtles lay their eggs on the beaches and Humpback Whales migrate close to the coast.

But it is the Whale Shark that has brought worldwide fame to Ningaloo. These magnificent fish can attain a length of 12m (40ft), making them the largest fish and

the largest cold-blooded animal in the world today. They have a distinctive checkerboard pattern of white spots and stripes that blend in beautifully with the ripples on the surface of the water.

Every autumn, after the corals spawn in March, Whale Sharks come into Ningaloo to feed on the plankton-rich soup. They are filter feeders that strain small organisms, such as krill, copepods and crab larvae, from the water. They also have up to 3000 small teeth that are thought to prevent larger prey such as squid, jelly-fish and small fish from slipping out of their enormous mouths.

Much research is being done at Ningaloo on Whale Sharks, yet we still know so little about them. Scientists still do not know where they spend the rest of the year after leaving Ningaloo, how long they live, or how many are alive throughout the world. Hopefully, with the information being obtained via current worldwide tag-ging programmes and studies, we will know a lot more about these magnificent animals in the near future.

OPPOSITE TOP *Divers should be aware of the massive, powerful tail as the animal swims by.*

OPPOSITE BOTTOM *A dive boat operator maintains radio commu-nication with a spotter plane as it looks for signs that a Whale Shark is in the vicinity. The divers enter the water ahead of the animal to view it as it passes.*

ABOVE *Wonderful sights like this are common at Ningaloo Reef during the Whale Shark season.*

AN INCOMPARABLE ENCOUNTER

Several of us slipped quietly off the diving platform at Ningaloo Reef and hovered in the warm water. We were waiting for the promised shadow of our first Whale Shark. It didn't take long. Within seconds, the shadow transformed into a gigantic mouth as the animal approached, swimming straight towards us. It was big; I remember thinking that two of us could fit into its mouth. It seemed oblivious to us, and hardly appeared to be moving, yet it was getting closer, quickly. I duck-dived down to take photos of its head. As I ascended, I moved to the side to avoid the mouth and passed closely beside the head. It was then that I realized that it wasn't oblivious to us. Its beady little eye watched me all the way, yet it never deviated in direction or movement. It was as if I was a tiny fly buzzing past an elephant.

Nothing quite compares to one's first encounter with an animal so large and powerful. Strict rules are in place at Ningaloo Reef to restrict the number of divers around a shark at one time, and they must be a certain distance from the animal. This is mainly to protect the Whale Sharks from being mobbed by over enthusiastic snorkellers. No scuba equipment or flash guns can be used but neither are necessary, as the sharks usually skim plankton from the surface, and many feed very slowly. Even so, with one flick of the tail they can dive to depths where scuba divers cannot follow. It is also worth remembering that accidents can occur, and the diver's safety is paramount. Once, when a friend of mine was involved in a tagging expedition, one of the tags was not embedded correctly so he had a second go at lodging the tag in the side of the shark. In one quick movement, the shark flicked him with its tail. He was bowled over but luckily did not lose consciousness, and escaped with a few broken ribs!

After one's first, mind-blowing encounter with a Whale Shark, it is worth observing the smaller, yet remarkable creatures that usually accompany these fish. There is often a Remora or two stuck to the shark's belly. An entourage of juvenile Golden Trevallies (Jacks) may be swimming around the mouth, waiting for morsels to be spat out by the giant, and large Cobia sometimes swim close by. It is also worth observing the water for other, not so friendly, sharks. From the surface, large Tiger Sharks have been mistaken for Whale Sharks, much to the horror of the first person in the water!

Ann Storrie, Animal technologist, diver and underwater photojournalist.
Wembly, Western Australia.

OPPOSITE *A snorkeller attaches a tag to a Whale Shark at Ningaloo Reef.*

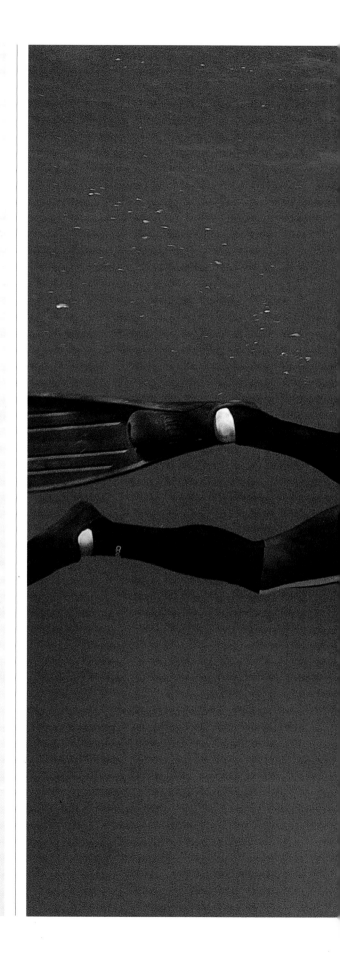

BASKING SHARKS

The common name, Basking Shark, is derived from the shark's habit of 'basking' at the surface, often lying with its back awash and dorsal fin high out of water, or on its side, or even on its back. When feeding at the surface Basking Sharks swim open-mouthed, and with the dorsal fin, upper lobe of the tail fin and sometimes the snout above water.

.The second largest fish in the sea after the Whale Shark, specimens can reach over 12m (40ft) long, with males reaching 6m (20ft) and females 12m (40ft), but 3–9m (10–30ft) is most common. Basking Sharks are among the most unusual sharks ever observed by divers. Due to their their shy nature and their habitat – in the dark, temperate waters of the world – they are seldom encountered underwater. However, when they are seen, they are dramatic and awe-inspiring; gigantic, gentle creatures that move through the water with their mouths agape.

The animal has extremely long gill slits, which almost meet above and below the throat, enabling the shark to feed and breathe simultaneously while swimming with its mouth wide open. The inner margin of each gill arch contains numerous horny, bristle-like rakers, directed inward, which act like giant filters and allow the water to pass through, but trap the plankton and funnel it toward the throat.

ABOVE *A Basking Shark scooping up plankton at the surface, with its massive mouth agape. Isle of Man.*
BELOW *It is common to see Basking Sharks with their upper fins breaking the surface, hence the name, basking. These animals are off California.*

Found mainly in cold and temperate waters, Basking Sharks usually occur singly or in small groups, but when there is an abundance of plankton, they congregate in large shoals. Like Whale Sharks, Basking Sharks are filter feeders, subsisting on tiny crustaceans, embryonic animals and eggs that float about in the planktonic soup that exists in large quantities in the cool oceans of the world. Feeding is a simple affair; they stretch their mouths open to a prodigious size, as much as 1m (3ft) across, then move through the water just below the surface. As the water passes over their gills, the mass of small organisms adheres to their gill rakers. The volume of food required to support these animals is large, and they may have half a tonne of food in their stomachs at any given time.

When feeding at the surface Basking Sharks are oblivious to boats, so they are easy to approach and dive with. A coxswain can motor the dive boat quietly ahead of the animal and be pretty sure that it will continue in the same straight line, so divers can quietly slip into the water while the boat is motored out of the way. Those in the water can see the massive dorsal fin approaching above the surface long before they can see the animal through the plankton soup. Suddenly they are aware that a huge gaping white mouth is almost on top of them and they have to be careful to get out of the way of the shark's large tail as it swings powerfully from side to side.

It is not worth trying to keep up with the fish by finning, so the encounter is over in seconds as the fish powers majestically on its way. However, where one Basking Shark is feeding at the surface there are usually many more, so the dive boat can pick up the divers and repeat the process several times until the divers are too tired to continue. They are not aggressive but they are large, powerful fish and like any large animal, should be treated with respect.

Basking Sharks can be a danger to small boats and, unusually among sharks, they breach, leaping wholly or partly out of the water like whales or dolphins.

Their habits are not yet well documented, and although they are occasionally seen in large shoals at certain times of the year when their preferred foods are plentiful, they disappear for four to five months each season. It is not known if they hibernate or merely change their feeding habits, sustaining themselves on small, deep-water organisms.

From Cornwall to the Clyde

Basking Sharks are frequently found off the western coast of Great Britain, although 1999 was an unusual year with reports of well in excess of 200 sharks at a time seen off the southern coast of the Lizard, Cornwall, peaking in May. Despite their large size, very little is known about their behaviour or ecology – not even where they come from, where they go to or how often they breed.

The first sightings of the year are off southwest England in early spring (March–April) and soon Basking Sharks are being sighted as far east as Shoreham in Sussex and all along the western coast, from Devon and Cornwall to the Firth of Clyde in Scotland; but by late autumn they have all disappeared again. The stomach contents of specimens that have been caught have been found to contain deep-water plankton. This, together with their large liver, high levels of squalene (a terpene found in the liver of sharks and most higher animals) and the fact that specimens caught in winter had no visible gill rakers or incompletely developed gill rakers has led to a suggestion of inactivity in deep waters when plankton levels are low.

ABOVE *Basking Sharks, powering along the surface scooping up plankton, are a common sight off the Isle of Man in the early spring.*

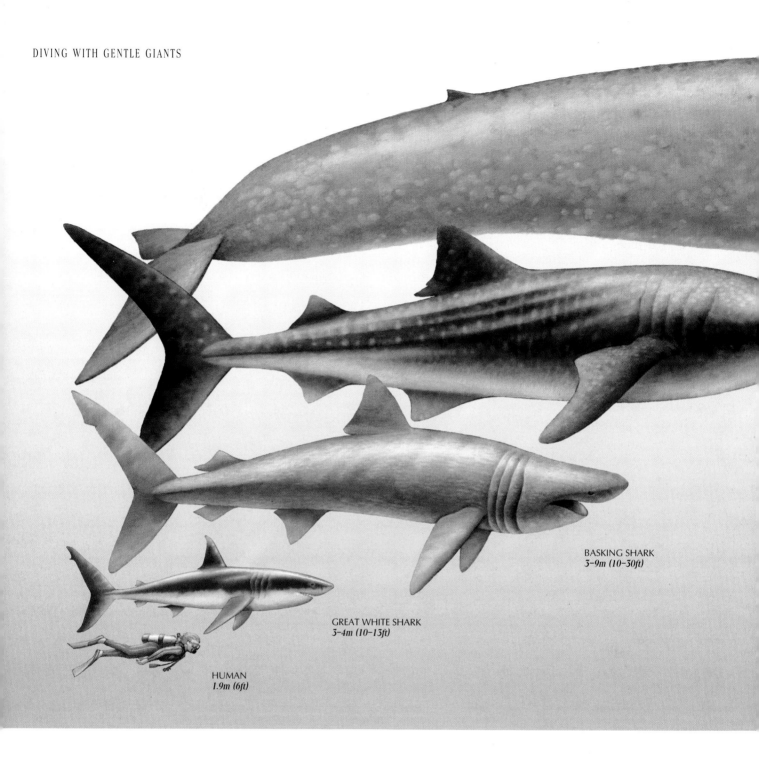

BASKING SHARK
3–9m (10–30ft)

GREAT WHITE SHARK
3–4m (10–13ft)

HUMAN
1.9m (6ft)

RIGHT *When feeding, the Basking Shark's huge mouth takes on awesome proportions.*

California

Basking Sharks appear off the coast of central and northern California in winter and early spring (November–April), when the cold Pacific water blooms with large quantities of plankton. Sometimes congregating in shoals of 60 or more, the sharks spend hour after hour swimming along the surface, straining the water for sustenance. At these times they can often be spotted with their dorsal (back) and caudal (tail) fins breaking the water while feeding.

Getting a clear view below water, however, is difficult due to their shy nature and the limited visibility of the often-green water as a result of the excess plankton during their prime feeding periods. Encounters require a great deal of patience – and a very warm wetsuit. Once Basking Sharks are spotted, divers can rely on their tendency to swim in a straight path. Divers on snorkel – the exhaust and noise from scuba regulators can frighten them – are dropped into the water well ahead of the shoal, but

BLUE WHALE
31m (100ft)

WHALE SHARK
10–12m (32–40ft)

SIZING UP

When set against the relative sizes of the sea's larger creatures, a diver's vulnerability becomes clear, particularly when taking into account that the underwater world is not man's natural environment.

in their path, to wait for them to swim past. Seeing and photographing these animals provides an eerie thrill as one floats in the ocean, far offshore, imagination racing while peering into the cold, dim water, able only to see a few metres in any direction.

When the sharks do appear, the sensation is breath-taking. The huge animals suddenly emerge from out of the gloom, moving at a speed of up to two knots, their prehistoric features and gigantic, white-lined mouths filling the scene, looking as if they could easily ingest every diver in the vicinity, fins and all.

DOLPHINS
RAYS
TURTLES &
JELLYFISH

AIR-BREATHING MAMMALS, DOLPHINS HAVE ALWAYS had a good relationship with people. They are readily observed breathing and breaching on the surface, riding the bow-wave of moving boats and often swimming close inshore. Lone male dolphins, ostracized from their group, even actively seek human company. Encounters with dolphins are high on most divers' wish lists.

Few communities fish dolphins for food, but large commercial fisheries have no sympathy when they get caught by long-lines and drift nets as a by-catch.

Where groups of wild dolphins interact with divers, they prefer people who keep moving and mimic dolphin behaviour, they do not like being touched. However, encounters with truly wild dolphins have not always been idyllic, there can be sharks in attendance and dolphins have been known to butt people if molested. Diving with dolphins should be treated as a privilege and, except in specific dolphinariums, they should not be touched.

Rays are related to sharks, have skeletons of cartilage, and use their greatly enlarged pectoral fins in a similar way to bird's wings to 'fly' through the water. Manta Rays can be 6.7m (22 ft) across, their size and grace making them a prime attraction. They are harmless and their tails do not have venomous barbs. In some parts of the world, local fishermen call them devilfish because of their habit of rubbing against anchor chains, causing them to drag. Curious of divers, Manta Rays will linger around them for long periods.

Diving specifically with stingrays is a relatively new phenomenon. When feeding, stingrays normally travel over the seabed using their Ampullae de Lorenzini receptors to locate prey, they respire (breathe) by drawing water through a small hole (the spiracle) behind the eye, and expelling it through their gill slits on the underside of their bodies to avoid getting sand in their gills.

Stingrays have venomous barbs at the base of their tails but these appear to be redundant in the modern world, as their predators – certain shark species – seem to be immune to them. When hand-fed by people, stingrays do not feel threatened, so there is little chance of divers being stung. Both Manta Rays and stingrays continue to be fished for food in many countries.

Marine turtles are air-breathing reptiles and an endangered species: Green Turtles are hunted for food, Hawksbill Turtles for tortoiseshell and Leatherback Turtles often mistake floating plastic bags for jellyfish prey, so that once swallowed, the indigestible plastic blocks their intestines, starving them to death. Turtles are caught in trawl nets, trammel nets, drift nets and long-lines, drowning from lack of air. Where divers can get up-close-and-personal with them, turtle-tourism may be the catalyst for their survival as they become more valuable alive than dead.

Finally, of the underwater world's smaller creatures, jellyfish are perhaps not the most interesting for a diver, nevertheless they can still provide an eerie, interesting interactive experience. They can range in size from tiny to many metres long; some have nasty, even deadly, stings, so divers should stay well clear if they are unsure of the species. Non-stinging jellyfish occuring in brackish lakes are a rarity and there are other rare creatures within these lakes so they attract recreational divers as well as marine biologists.

DOLPHINS
RAYS
TURTLES &
JELLYFISH

PREVIOUS PAGES *Dolphins are among the most-loved marine mammals, and few divers would not relish the opportunity to swim with them in their natural environment. This pod of Atlantic Spotted Dolphins was photographed off the Bahamas.*

OPPOSITE *A turtle heads to the surface for air.*

ABOVE *Snorkelling among jellyfish has been described as an eerie experience.*

TOP RIGHT *Potato Cod are generally docile and often inquisitive, and will often approach divers and swim alongside them.*

BOTTOM RIGHT *Stingrays often jostle divers in their search for food, but the intense suction their feeding action generates can leave bruises, or 'hickies' on the skin.*

DIVING WITH DOLPHINS

Most divers' encounters with dolphins are little more than a fleeting glimpse in the water overhead as a group noisily passes, but some have accepted the close presence of people in the water. Most habituated dolphins are Bottlenose Dolphins, either semi-captive or lone males looking for company and not too worried about divers' noisy exhaust bubbles. The Atlantic Spotted Dolphins off the Bahamas are truly wild animals; those at White Sand Ridge, Grand Bahama, are well-known but operators are now finding other friendly groups, particularly in the Bahamas. When divers interact with wild dolphins, they should always watch out for dangerous sharks, especially when the encounter is over deep water.

Dolphin Reef, Eilat, Israel

Dolphin Reef, at Eilat on the Israeli Red Sea, comprises one hectare (2.5 acres) of sheltered sea, enclosed with buoyed nets and reaching a depth of 18m (60ft). This is home to a group of Bottlenose Dolphins; some of which were rescued from Russia and Japan. Despite their different geographic origins, they seem to be quite happy living as one boisterous group, the females regularly becoming pregnant and giving birth. The dolphins can jump the net to freedom, and often do, usually returning some time later with fresh propeller scars on their backs from encounters with boats.

Divers feel it is a great privilege to experience the dolphins at Dolphin Reef. They will enter the enclosure full of anticipation – they can hear the clicks and shrieks of the dolphins' echo-location – but at first they cannot see them. Suddenly two or more dolphins will speed into view, a vision of graceful

BELOW *Bottlenose Dolphins at Dolphin Reef, Eilat, Gulf of Aqaba, Red Sea.*

beauty rushing up to the divers and coming to a halt, peering quizzically into their face masks, just inches away from their faces.

Recognizing the accompanying staff divemaster, they will search him or her for food. They are extremely playful creatures, and will seek out the baseball cap that the divemaster hides in a BCD pocket, and play with it like children with a ball.

After tiring of playing, they will move away, but soon dash back again, passing by and then beneath the divemaster, twisting onto their backs and inviting him to scratch their stomachs. More dolphins will suddenly arrive (the group can number 10 or more) and they will begin to interact, playfully twirling and tumbling around with lots of noise, touching each other or nosing each other's fins in friendship. Some dolphins burrow in the sand for prey, mothers suckle their calves, while others play with bits of seaweed, passing it to each other – and even to the divers, as if asking them to join in the fun.

It is impossible to know what a dolphin is thinking about when it peers into your face-mask. Is it looking at its own reflection, is it treating you as a friend or is it using echo-location on a frequency that you cannot hear to 'look' deeper into your body as it does through the sand in the quest for prey. There have been several recorded cases where lone male Bottlenose Dolphins have sought out human company and reacted sexually so it is likely that their response to interaction with swimmers and divers is favourable so long as they are not harassed.

Dolphins have always been perceived as 'cuddly' creatures, although recent research has found that some dolphin species kill smaller species. Many experts believe that patients suffering from depression and mental illness experience an uplifting effect when they swim with dolphins, so Dolphin Reef is fully equipped to deal with those who have special needs, including the blind and those normally confined to wheelchairs.

During the day the dolphins see hundreds of divers and snorkellers, so they could be forgiven for becoming bored with them; it is best to book the first dive of the day for the best visibility and the fact that the dolphins have not had human contact overnight, so they are likely to be more curious.

There are those who object to habituating wild animals or keeping them in enclosures, but on a positive note, the dolphins are not forced to interact with people and, for children in particular, the creatures of Dolphin Reef provide an effective way of instilling a strong message of conservation.

ABOVE LEFT *The coral reef beach and aquarium complex at Eilat, on the Israeli Red Sea.*

ABOVE CENTRE *Snorkelling with Bottlenose Dolphins at Dolphin Reef, on the Gulf of Aqaba, Israel.*

ABOVE RIGHT *Coral World Aquarium and underwater observatory at Eilat, Gulf of Aqaba, Israel.*

BELOW *A Bottlenose Dolphin attempts to steal a divermaster's baseball cap at Dolphin Reef, Eilat.*

ABOVE *Children enjoying the show at a Dolphin Education Centre in Freeport, Bahamas.*

BELOW *Although the habituated dolphins are happy to frolic with divers off Grand Bahama, it is the food handouts that are the incentive.*

White Sand Ridge and Sanctuary Bay, Bahamas

Grand Bahama Island lies off the coast of southern Florida, about 110km (70 miles) east of West Palm Beach. The Gulf Stream originates in deep water off the coast of Mexico, where it is heated by the tropical sun and pushed north by the trade winds. Carrying marine life from the Caribbean into the Atlantic Ocean, the Gulf Stream acts as a barrier, protecting the Bahamas from Florida's rain and river runoff. This, together with bottomless oceanic trenches that allow sediment to settle into deep water, ensures good visibility unless there is rough weather. The Bahama Banks plateau, rising from deep water to 3m (10 feet) from the surface, acts as a breeding and feeding ground for prolific marine life.

North of Grand Bahama's West End, White Sand Ridge has clear water over a white sandy bottom 3–9m (10–30ft) deep. A plentiful food supply and relatively few predators make it a favourite place for dolphin mothers with calves. A live-aboard only destination, divers encounter groups of six to 40 Atlantic Spotted Dolphins at White Sand Ridge. When large groups occur and the visibility is good, divers in the water can see as many as 16 dolphins at a time: adults, youngsters and even mothers with calves (during the calving season in spring and autumn). They root in the sand for crustaceans and flounders, squabble among themselves, assist each other after birth and interact with or fight off Bottlenose Dolphins or sharks. The dolphins often approach within touching distance of divers and stare into their eyes, there is a lot of swimming upside down and sometimes they stay around the boat for hours, frequently for most of night.

For many years resident pods of Spotted Dolphins on White Sand Ridge have been happy to accept the close company of humans and even to interact with them, especially if they mimic dolphin behaviour. Dive operators have perfected the art of locating the dolphins, circling their boats to attract them to the bow-waves that they love to ride and then stopping. Surprisingly most of the animals do not swim off when the boats stop, so clients can join them in the water though it is hard to keep up with them when swimming against the current. As with Manta Rays, dolphins prefer snorkellers to divers, possibly the noisy exhaust bubbles from scuba equipment upsets them.

Frolicking with these wonderful creatures and the excitement of being accepted by highly intelligent wild animals in their own environment is a rewarding experience. Many divers will feel just as much satisfaction from interacting with dolphins as they would from diving with sharks. Most films depicting Atlantic Spotted Dolphin behaviour in the wild were taken here and star these animals.

On an easier level, one can interact with habituated Atlantic Bottlenose Dolphins at Dolphin Experience in Sanctuary Bay, on the southwest end of Grand Bahama. This highly successful programme combines an educational encounter for snorkellers and swimmers in swimming pool-like conditions in the bay, plus the chance to swim with these dolphins 1.6km (one mile) offshore.

At Dolphin Experience, divers settle on sand at 15m (50 ft) and staff pilot a small boat towards them with trained dolphins swimming alongside. You first hear their echo-location sonar pings and whistles, then they appear, swim up to the divers, stare into their masks and seemingly pose for the cameras. Occasionally they are joined by pods of genuinely wild dolphins so divers can enjoy the sight of wild Atlantic Spotted Dolphins swimming with habituated Atlantic Bottlenose Dolphins.

ABOVE *Interaction with wild dolphins is an unforgettable experience for most divers. The dolphins of the Bahamas are world-renowned due to the many wildlife films in which they have featured.*

LEFT *Regular contact with the dolphins enables dive operators to build up relationships with individual animals.*

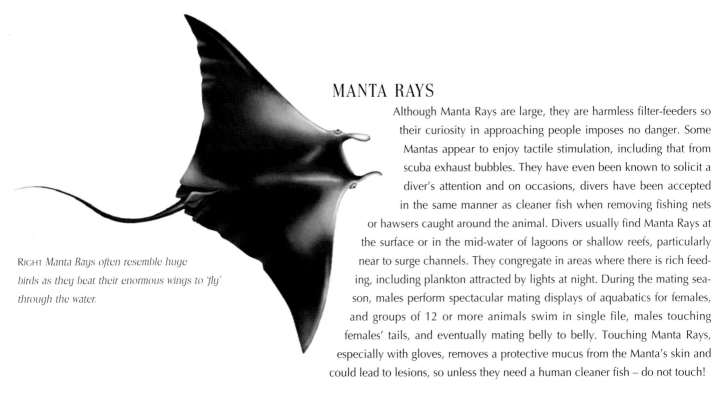

MANTA RAYS

Although Manta Rays are large, they are harmless filter-feeders so their curiosity in approaching people imposes no danger. Some Mantas appear to enjoy tactile stimulation, including that from scuba exhaust bubbles. They have even been known to solicit a diver's attention and on occasions, divers have been accepted in the same manner as cleaner fish when removing fishing nets or hawsers caught around the animal. Divers usually find Manta Rays at the surface or in the mid-water of lagoons or shallow reefs, particularly near to surge channels. They congregate in areas where there is rich feeding, including plankton attracted by lights at night. During the mating season, males perform spectacular mating displays of aquabatics for females, and groups of 12 or more animals swim in single file, males touching females' tails, and eventually mating belly to belly. Touching Manta Rays, especially with gloves, removes a protective mucus from the Manta's skin and could lead to lesions, so unless they need a human cleaner fish – do not touch!

RIGHT *Manta Rays often resemble huge birds as they beat their enormous wings to 'fly' through the water.*

BELOW *Manta Rays often interact with each other, particularly during the mating season when the males perform spectacular courtship displays for the females.*

Valley of the Rays, Yap, Micronesia

Up close and personal is the best way to describe Manta Ray encounters at Yap, one of the four island clusters making up the Caroline Islands, part of Micronesia, in the Pacific Ocean. The Manta Rays glide so close to divers' heads that they duck down involuntarily, while some individual animals seem to enjoy a bath of scuba exhaust bubbles on their bellies, which may feel like the action of cleaner fish to them.

Yap has two surge channels, through opposite sides of the fringing reef, which concentrate plankton where the channels become narrow and shallow. These, combined with the prevalent weather pattern, allow diving with Manta Rays all year round. The animals move regularly into these channels for feeding and cleaning. In the mating season, from December to late April, a succession of up to 18 Mantas cruise the Mi'l channel into Manta Ray Bay on the west side of the reef. In the summer season they are found on Yap's eastern side at Goofnuw channel in the Valley of the Rays. Here the Manta Rays are less engaged in cleaning activity so they move around more and the divers can get away from each other.

Schools of Manta Rays come in to the channels almost every morning as the tides turn so these dives are dependant on the tide, both for getting to the sites over the shallow lagoon and for finding the best visibility, which occurs towards the end of a flood (incoming) tide. This may mean that prospective divers have to set out at dawn.

The divers may still be sleepy when they reach Mi'l channel but they are wide awake as soon as they hit the water. Escorted by dive guides they will take up positions on the sand behind various coral heads at around 15m (50ft) and wait quietly for the Manta Rays to appear. If they have got the state of the tide right Mi'l channel can have 30m (100ft) visibility over the 8m (25ft) ledge called Manta Ridge, though 9–12m (30–40ft) is more common.

Manta Rays resemble huge birds, beating their wings and 'flying' through the water. They do not have true wings but a pair of greatly enlarged pectoral fins that can be operated independently, giving skillful manoeuvrability. Their long tails, stretching out 2–2.5m (6–8ft) behind them, do not have a sting.

Several Manta Rays are likely to be in line, head to tail, twisting and turning as they glide past the divers. Then they break formation and each heads for its favourite cleaning station where it acts as if in a trance while butterflyfish, damselfish and wrasse swim out from the coral and dart in and out of their mouths and gills picking off parasites and dead skin.

After the divers have rested, a second dive – a drift dive with the tide along Mi'l channel towards the open sea – will produce all the normal Pacific marine life, but Manta Rays seem to be everywhere. The local divemasters have so far identified more than 45 separate animals by their markings.

In the mating season groups of Manta Rays perform a courtship display of awe-inspiring in-water aquabatics. One after another they forge ahead at high speed, rolling, dipping and soaring – a spectacular, sensuous and frenzied dance displaying aquatic proficiency that divers can only dream about. Males will follow females, touching their tails and if one is receptive, will mate with her.

The Manta Rays of Yap are not tame but they have become used to the nonintrusive presence of humans and will approach within touching distance. However they cannot reverse and, if frightened they may bolt, so, considering their size, it is well not to spook them.

Top *The beach at Yap.*
Above *Yap Divers' dive boats at their jetty.*
Left *Up close and personal. Manta Rays will approach divers if they are not harassed.*
Below *A Manta Ray glides over the reef to its favourite cleaning station, where reef fish remove parasites and dead skin.*

Sandy Ridge, Sangalaki, Kalimantan

The Kepulauan Sangalaki Marine Wildlife Reserve, which lies on the edge of Kalimantan's continental shelf, is a 280ha (690-acre) marine park surrounding the tiny island of Sangalaki (Pulau Sangalaki). It is one of a remote group of islands that include Kakaban and Samama, 50km (30 miles) east of the Berau River estuary in Kalimantan (Indonesian Borneo). Two of the larger islands, Pulau Derawan and Pulau Maratua, are inhabited by the Dayak people and Bajau sea gypsies, while the rest are uninhabited except when tourists are on Sangalaki.

The islands are very close to the Wallace Line, a hypothetical zoological dividing line charted by the English naturalist Alfred Russell Wallace, which runs through the Makassar Strait between Borneo and Sulawesi (also called Celebes). This line denotes a biogeographical transition zone with fundamental zoological differences occuring on either side of it between the animal species of Asia and those of Australia.

When divers sit calmly and quietly at 15m (50ft) on the undulating sandy bottom of Sangalaki's Sandy Ridge, they are constantly dive bombed by at least 20 Manta Rays in convoy (over 100 different Manta Rays are claimed to have been seen on one dive). The animals seem to be circling because the same ones come back time and again. In general they are not as large as the lone individuals seen elsewhere; 3–4m (10–13ft) across is common, but they come in very close. They do not appear to be attempting to drive divers out of their territory, they are just being curious.

Snorkelling with the Manta Rays is equally rewarding, as they tend to feed near the surface in light currents and give snorkellers even more attention than they give to divers, returning again and again to check them out. Sometimes one has to take evasive action to get out of their way for fear of a collision.

At Sandy Ridge other attractions such as the cuttlefish, Garden Eels and ever present massive Green Turtles take second place to the Manta Rays. When there is a strong current running, divers can string out while holding on to a rope attached to an old anchor, but they must beware of the stinging hydroids and sharp juvenile shellfish found on the rope.

Lone, large Manta Rays, measuring up to 6m (20ft) across, can be found anywhere in the area, often approaching boats near to the island, and they are curiously unsuspecting of snorkellers. However, the smaller Manta Rays congregate across the north of the island. Travelling from west to east, Manta Run, Manta Parade and Manta Avenue are all dive sites just 10 minutes by speedboat from the Sangalaki resort's beach, where shoals of up to 50 Manta Rays promenade up and down, mouths wide open, feeding on a rich supply of plankton.

During the November to March rainy season, visibility can be below 10m (33ft), as runoff from the nearby Berau River contains silt from logging, but after a few dry days it can average 30m (100ft).

Sangalaki is a great diving destination – with turtles similar to Sipadan, Manta Rays similar to Yap (though not so large), Kakaban's walls, Hammerhead Sharks and a brackish lake (an ancient caldera containing four species of nonstinging jellyfish and jellyfish-eating anemones). Unlike Palau, these jellyfish have not been affected by high temperatures from the recent El Niño. The only drawback is the long journey to get there, but hopefully this will limit divers from flocking there in large numbers and negatively affecting the local ecology.

OPPOSITE Manta Rays are more curious of snorkellers at the surface than divers and will return several times if the snorkeller does not chase after them.
ABOVE Snorkelling over a reef at Sangalaki Marine Reserve.
BELOW A Manta Ray feeding at the surface. The horns on either side of the head funnel plankton into the cavernous mouth.

Sanganeb, Red Sea, Sudan

Sanganeb Reef lies 27km (17 miles) northeast of Port Sudan. Approaching Sanganeb's Southwest Point on a windy December or January day can be fraught with difficulty for dive boat skippers. Manta Rays seem to be on the surface everywhere and skippers must juggle to safely moor the boat in the strong wind without injuring any of the Mantas with the boat's propellers. Once moored, the Manta Rays swimming around the boat become the divers' problem, and they have to ensure that their entry into the water is clear so that they do not land on a creature when they jump off the boat.

In the water, divers often find that when Manta Rays congregate in groups they are both curious and fearless. The visibility is poor, resulting from a combination of the heavily choppy surface caused by the wind, together with the plankton and sediment washed off the reef, so when two or three Manta Rays regularly appear together out of the gloom, it is quite a sight. Reaching 3–4.5m (10–15ft) across, even their accompanying remoras are nearly 1m (3ft) long.

Most of these animals remain around one reef all year so long as there is enough food and a mate. Sanganeb is a very large reef and its southern end consists of a long wall, which in the windy months is in the lee of the constant north wind, the only place on the reef where the animals can feed on plankton at the surface. All of the Manta Rays here have markings that make them recognizable as permanent residents of Sanganeb. Like the resident shoal of dolphins, rays congregate here to feed comfortably at the surface when the sea elsewhere around the reef is too rough. There is a similar congregation of other Manta Rays and dolphins off the south end of nearby Wingate Reefs in December and January. At other times of the year the Mantas are spread out singly around Red Sea reefs, over shallow shelves or in protected reef lagoons, often feeding on the surface from midday to early evening.

Unlike in the Maldives and at Yap, no permanent Manta cleaning stations in surge channels have been observed in the Red Sea, nor do any dive resorts entice Manta Rays by attracting plankton with lights at night. One individual ray is often encountered being cleaned at around 10m (33ft) over the first step off the North Point of Sanganeb. When divers appear, it will often stop being cleaned and go into a series of somersaults in front of them. An interesting display that occurs regularly off Sanganeb's South Jetty and Towartit's Harvey Reef is lone animals leaping out of the sea two or three times in succession, each time falling back into the water with a loud slap.

Aggregations of 15 or so Manta Rays occur in August in the shallow waters around Mesharifa and Gad Mesherifa Islets east of Sudan's Muhammad Qõl. In nearby Dungûnab Bay the surface is calm, so it is believed, but not proven, that the bay is used for mating. One rarely encounters very small juvenile rays; they remain in protected shallow waters that divers do not dive in, but tiny individuals, not much more than 30cm (1ft) across are often seen leaping out of the water in Port Sudan harbour, despite the pollution.

Manta Rays are a common sight in the central and northern Red Sea. They are not fished in Egyptian, Israeli or Sudanese waters so their curiousity has not been affected. If approached slowly and quietly by snorkel rather than on noisy scuba equipment, they will hang around divers and often return to them. Further south, however, where they are fished, they are more wary.

STINGRAYS

Diving with stingrays at Grand Cayman and Gibb's Cay on Grand Turk, in the Caribbean, are fun dives that change people's attitudes in a positive way and save the rays from being killed wastefully. Although they are happy to accept handouts, they are still observed hunting naturally, delving in the sand for prey. Be aware that the animals become boisterous in their search for food but none have ever attacked divers or snorkellers. To avoid damage to their skin, do not wear gloves.

Stingray City, Grand Cayman

At Stingray City, Southern Stingrays follow the sound of any approaching boat's engine and as soon as it is anchored they converge from all directions and gather around seeking a free lunch. This one of the Caribbean's most famous underwater attractions, and the site is probably dived or snorkelled by more people than any other site in the world. The first time that people participate in this dive, it can be a little frightening. The stingrays actually nudge and jostle divers boisterously while flapping around, sometimes bumping into face masks in their search for food.

The stingrays are dark grey, brown or black on top, and white underneath. Adult females can be 2m (6ft) across but most of those found here are smaller males. They have broad, flat bodies with small barely-defined heads. Used to searching for their prey in the sand they have eyes on top of their bodies but their mouths are set back underneath their bodies. They cannot see their prey but sense food with a combination of highly developed receptors – smell and touch – then

Opposite At Sanganeb, where a combination sediment washed off the reef and plankton results in poor visibility in December and January, a large, lone Manta Ray emerging from the gloom can be an awesome sight.

Above Stingrays use their sense of smell and touch to search the sandy seabed for food, which they suck into their mouths using two hard dental plates.

suck food into their mouths between two hard dental plates. They are often confused by the scent of several people carrying food in the water and begin sucking as they approach what they think is the source of the food. This can result in uncomfortable 'hickies' – suction marks on people's skin similar to love bites. For this reason, and the high chance of sunburn in such shallow water, it is wise to wear a skin suit or light wet suit.

Stingray City lies just inside a natural channel passing through the barrier reef on the northwest corner of Grand Cayman's North Sound. The channel is 3.5–5.5m (12–18ft) deep and has a flat sandy base with solitary coral heads – an ideal place for stingrays to search for food in the sand. Generations of Cayman fishermen used to anchor in this sheltered spot to clean and fillet their catch before landing it. They threw the waste overboard and over the years, stingrays got used to this plentiful supply of food. When the site was 'discovered' in summer 1986 by two local divemasters, news got out to an American diving magazine and they sent a writer-photographer down in 1987 to do a story. She coined the name 'Stingray City' while her editor invented the headline 'the world's best 3.5m (12ft) dive'. Since then, scores of divers have experienced the thrill of hand-feeding the many Stingrays that congregate here. Nowadays there is also a similar site called Sandbar near Rum Point channel, which is only waist deep.

Boat skippers give clients pieces of chopped up squid and if they keep the food in their closed fist the rays can be led around following the scent, though people may get jostled by another stingray approaching from another direction. When the divers wish to feed the stingrays, they should open their fist and keep their fingers straight, pointed away from the hand so that their palm is flat and bent backward. Stingrays do not have teeth but can generate the suction of a vacuum cleaner.

They are bottom dwellers, feeding primarily on molluscs and crustaceans in the sand, so one cannot simply just release the fish into the water as the stingrays cannot catch it. If divers do release the bait into the water it is most likely to be taken by one of the many smaller fish, such as Yellowtail Snappers or Sergeant Majors, that are always present.

Once the feeding session is over, the rays slow down and become more docile. This is a good time to take photographs if the divers and stingrays have not stirred up the sand too much.

OPPOSITE *Divers can enjoy interacting with Southern Stingrays at Stingray City, Grand Cayman.*
LEFT *Southern Stingrays naturally swim close to the sand.*
TOP *Local snorkel boats converge on the Sandbar each day to play with the resident stingrays in the shallow waters off Grand Cayman Island.*
BELOW *Although female Stingrays can be 2m (6ft) across, most of those found at Stingray City are smaller males. The diver gives some idea of the scale of the Stingray.*

ABOVE Green Turtles can be found mating for up to two hours.
BELOW Hatchlings, such as these Green Turtle hatchlings on Sangalaki, face many risks before they make it to the relative safety of the sea.
OPPOSITE When photographing turtles and other marine animals, divers must ensure that they don't allow any part of their bodies or equipment to touch the coral.

TURTLES

Turtles go back over 150 million years, to the age of the dinosaurs. Having changed little in their evolutionary history, they still closely resemble their fossil ancestors and can live for more than 100 years. Of the seven species of marine turtles in the world's oceans, six are found in the Pacific. The two most commonly encountered at Sipadan and Sangalaki are Green and Hawksbill Turtles. Both species appear to be a mottled dull-green underwater but adult Green Turtles reach a length of 1.2m (4ft) compared to the smaller Hawksbill's 84cm (33in). In young Hawksbills, the plates of the carapace (shell) overlap, but in adults they merely adjoin and are the characteristic tortoiseshell brown colour with yellow markings. Hawksbill Turtles have a distinct beak while the outer edge of their carapace is usually jagged.

Sipadan and Sangalaki

Viewing turtles is a highlight for most divers but the huge aggregations of nesting turtles that used to occur yearly on many beaches in warmer parts of the world are things of the past. All turtles are now on the endangered species list and divers feel privileged if they spot one; however at Pulau Sipadan and Pulau Sangalaki, two islands off the coast of Kalimantan (Borneo), turtle encounters are guaranteed. Massive 136–181kg (300–400 lb) Green Turtles and smaller Hawksbill Turtles gather off these islands to mate and nest while the occasional Pacific Olive Ridley Turtle passes by. Habituated to divers, the turtles are almost tame and carry on with life as though divers were just another marine inhabitant that posed no threat.

At some dive sites, 20–30 turtles can be encountered, engaged in the serious business of eating, sleeping, being cleaned of algae by herbivorous surgeonfish, using the coral to scratch parasites off their carapace, or mating. Hawksbill Turtles may be watched as they feed on sponges, or Green Turtles may be found sleeping.

Mating is a rough experience for both male and female turtles. As soon as one male begins to copulate with a female, many others bite his flippers and try to pull him away so that they can take his place. Turtles need to breathe air and it is quite common to find a female struggling to reach the surface to breathe while weighed down by six or more desperate suitors. The whole process can take more than two hours, which is why many Asians consider turtle meat and eggs to have the properties of an aphrodisiac.

Roughly six times a season, when the tide is high at night, female turtles haul themselves laboriously up the beaches to nest. Each clears a nesting site with sweeping motions of her front flippers and digs a body cavity in which to deposit her eggs, often digging up a previous turtle's eggs in the process. After laying their eggs the females try to fill in the cavity with sand, though they rarely make a good job of concealing the nest. When heading back to the sea, their desire to reach its safety after two laborious hours of nesting causes them to climb desperately over anything that is in their way, even if they could easily pass around it, and especially if dawn is already breaking. This regularly occurs in front of the divers' accommodation so they get a grandstand seat. About two months later the hatchlings break their way out of the sand and run the gauntlet of predators to the sea.

On both islands the income generated from international diving clients has enabled the dive operators to stop the collection of turtle eggs for food, and on Sipadan, wildlife rangers operate a turtle hatchery. The freshly laid eggs are quickly

excavated and transplanted by hand into a wired-off pit where, once they have hatched, they can be counted and then released safely into the sea at night.

To the west of the jetty at Pulau Sipadan, there is a deep wall with several small caves in the top 10m (33ft), where Green Turtles are often found sleeping next to Bumphead Parrotfish at night. To the east of the jetty, at 18m (60ft), a much larger cave is the entrance to the famous Turtle Cavern (see page 146) where many turtles have become lost in the interconnecting passages and drowned.

Although there are other islands off Kalimantan where turtles nest, their offshore topography is not good for diving, so to divers, Pulau Sipadan and Pulau Sangalaki are the turtle capitals of the world.

BELOW LEFT *A female Green Turtle glides gracefully through the water at Sipadan.*
BELOW RIGHT *Hawksbill Turtles are the smallest of the marine turtles, easily recognized by their bird-like beak.*

ABOVE *Kakaban's Jellyfish Lake viewed from the air.*
RIGHT *A snorkeller swims over a bed of Halimeda algae (seaweed) at Jellyfish Lake, Kakaban*

JELLYFISH

Jellyfish can appear seasonally in areas of calm, shallow water. Many of those occurring in the sea can inflict painful stings, some of which can be fatal. They are pelagic animals, made up of an umbrella-shaped bell with tentacles trailing beneath. Stinging cells on the tentacles enable the jellyfish to stun and trap prey. As with anemones, tiny juvenile fish sheltering among the tentacles are not troubled by the stinging cells. Although capable of movement, jellyfish are generally carried along with ocean currents. Barely denser than the surrounding water, they maintain their position in the water column by rhythmic pulsations of their bell, tending to sink when pulsation stops. They spread their tentacles in the capture of prey. Jellyfish trapped in landlocked lakes no longer have predators or prey that are affected by stinging cells, so these have died out and the animals have evolved other means of feeding.

Jellyfish Lake, Kakaban

The island of Kakaban, off Kalimantan (Indonesian Borneo), is an unusual marine environment. During the Holocene period, 20,000 years ago, upliftment in the area left a huge seawater lake trapped inland. The only other landlocked lakes of this nature are found on islands in the Palau (Belau) group in Micronesia, but those lakes are deserts when compared to the one on Kakaban.

Over thousands of years, the inhabitants of this lake have adapted to what is now a brackish water environment with a limited range of predators. The lake is teeming with at least four species of jellyfish that no longer need to have stinging cells, including one of the upside-down Cassiopeia species. Some of the jellyfish sink to the bottom where, in the grassy areas, white anemones have evolved to feed on them. The lake is surrounded by mangroves whose roots are encrusted with sponges. Unidentified species are common; at least three types of Halimeda green algae species exist on the bottom, together with tube worms, shrimps, sea cucumbers, sea snakes and five types of Goby (small fish).

Pulau Kakaban, which is about 25 minutes by boat from Sangalaki, is relatively large but not suitable for habitation. The lake covers most of the island and is big enough for several islands the size of Sangalaki to fit into. To reach the lake, the trail begins from the shore near to the centre of Kakaban's southern bay and divers must trek through a narrow strip of jungle. Unlike on Palau, where a long trek to the lake restricts divers to snorkelling, on Kakaban the staff at Borneo Divers have improved the track and provide porters to help divers carry their equipment so that they can scuba dive if they wish to. The path climbs up over a ridge before it descends to the lake, and when wet, it can be slippery so it is advisable to wear sandals or trainers.

The deepest part of the lake is about 10m (33ft) and in places the jellyfish are so thick that divers cannot see through them and are constantly bumping into them. One's natural instincts make it difficult to remember that the jellyfish cannot sting. Although most clients snorkel, for photography purposes, it is worth taking a small scuba cylinder and diving equipment.

Even when they do not sting, swimming through millions of jellyfish is not to everyone's taste. However, the jellyfish here have not been decimated by El Niño, like those in Palau, so the experience is a unique one.

ABOVE *Tourists returning from Jellyfish Lake.*
BELOW LEFT *Species new to science, such as this Goby (Cristagobius), are continually being found in Jellyfish Lake.*
BELOW RIGHT *An under-over view showing the mangroves that surround Kakaban's Jellyfish Lake.*

Jellyfish Lake, Palau

Palau is one of the Caroline Islands (part of Micronesia, now the Independent Republic of Belau), situated in the western Pacific Ocean. It is a breathtaking vista from the air, with hundreds of emerald-green mushroom-shaped islands dotted in a 140km–long (90-mile) turquoise lagoon. Jungle-covered, with steep vertical sides, these are the legendary Rock Islands. Fringing the lagoon, a barrier reef protects the 328 islands from large ocean swells and stormy seas.

The extraordinary marine world of Palau has been widely acclaimed as one of the seven underwater wonders of the world. Jellyfish Lake on the island of Eil Malk offers a thrilling and mysterious dive adventure. The best-known of several marine lakes in Palau, it was created millions of years ago by a geological upheaval that lifted and reshaped countless reefs, trapping and imprisoning the ocean within lush miniature lakes. They are surrounded by land, but are fed sea water through cracks and fissures in the island's limestone base. The majority of these lakes are still unexplored. Some are said to be as hot as 37°C (98°F), some to be inhabited by saltwater crocodiles. Some hold life forms that are found nowhere else on earth.

The Jellyfish Lake experience comes with a price tag. It begins with a hike up a jungle hillside on an isolated rocky island, carrying camera equipment and film in a watertight bag. The guides make sure nothing superfluous is carried, even towels often remain on the boat, replaced by an effective, handkerchief-sized chamois. The hike is not overly strenuous, but it is steep, hot and very humid. Adequate sun protection is essential. It is also advisable to wear hard-soled dive bootees to protect your feet from the razor-sharp limestone rocks. The trail is interspersed with

trees that have a powerful stinging sap, and an experienced guide is essential to point out the route. After the descent, a wade and swim through a mangrove creek finally brings one to the warm saltwater lake. A good guide knows where the jelly-fish are massing in relation to the time of day to allow divers the full experience of the dense shoals – both for the tactile sensation and the photographic opportunities.

Scientists believe that prior to the last El Niño, there were as many as two mil-lion of the small, pulsating Mastigias Jellyfish, a subspecies of their ocean-dwelling cousins, in this lake alone. In the absence of predators and a constant food supply from the ocean larder, the creatures were forced to adapt and evolve, leading to a redundancy in defence and food-trapping mechanisms, such as stinging tentacles. Instead, microscopic algae cells that could produce food were courted.

With the jellyfish being dependent on the sun for the process of photosynthesis, these algae cells cause the mysterious daily mass migration of their hosts across the lake as they follow the path of the sun, travelling almost 1.5km (1 mile) each day.

Divers describe swimming amidst the pulsing jellyfish as an eerie experience, a combination of sensations; from wading and sliding through a solid wall of crea-tures, to the soft, quivering bumps of individual jellyfish colliding with the body.

The dives are undertaken with snorkels, as it is rather cumbersome to drag scuba gear up the incline. Scuba diving can be arranged, but only with a permit and specialist guide – necessary due to noxious bottom-water layers that call for strict depth limits. The isolated and undisturbed water is separated into three dis-tinct layers. The first is the sea-water layer containing both Mastigias Jellyfish and a small layer of elegant Moon Jellies. The second layer, at 20m (65ft), is milky-red, created by billions of nitrogen-rich bacteria. At night, the jellyfish migrate down to the final, third layer to feed and fertilize in a zone of nitrogen-rich bacteria and hydrogen sulphide, both of which are highly toxic. For the jellyfish it is a brief journey and they soon rise to the surface to await daybreak. For the diver, howev-er, even a few moments in this layer could be fatal.

Traditionally, several of Palau's marine lakes are closed at certain times of the year to allow the smaller jellyfish to grow. However, the higher than usual water temperatures caused by the last El Niño resulted in the widespread destruction of the jellyfish and Palau's famous lakes may be closed for some years, so it is wise to check in advance with local dive shops before planning a trip.

OPPOSITE TOP *A diver moves tentatively through the non-stinging jellyfish in Eil Malk Lake, Palau*
OPPOSITE BOTTOM *Mastigias and Moon jellyfish in Eil Malk Lake, Palau before the 1997/98 El Niño. Since then virtually all the jellyfish have died but the authorities are attempting to restock the lake with a few from elsewhere and hope that they will reproduce over time.*
ABOVE LEFT *A Moon Jellyfish in Eil Malk Lake, Palau.*
ABOVE RIGHT *Palau's scenic Rock Islands from the air.*

ABOVE *Eels and Potato Cod are both known to be curious and will allow allow divers to get close to them, but divers should resist the temptation to touch the animals and should always respect their space.*

BELOW *Potato Cod exhibit a courtship display.*

OTHER MARINE ANIMALS

Although underwater photographers are enthused by small creatures, especially in low-visibility 'muck diving', most divers are interested in larger animals they can get close to, such as large groupers, which can be over 2m (6ft), and Giant Humphead (Napoleon) Wrasse. Both species are sitting targets for spearfishing and live Napoleons are desired by the Southeast Asian restaurant trade, so they have been decimated, although small numbers can be found at sites where they are protected.

Potato Cod, Ningaloo Reef, Western Australia

Potato Cod is the name given to a type of very large grouper found in tropical Australian waters. A fearless predator, preying on smaller fish, they grow to 1.4m (55in) in length and can weigh over 62kg (139 lb). Distinguished by potato-sized dark blotches over the body, head and fins, the Potato Cod's large, fleshy lips hide rows of tiny, needle-sharp teeth.

Potato Cod are usually found on coral reefs where they like to frequent large caves and crevices. They are common on outer reefs, such as the Rowley Shoals, off Broome in Western Australia, or Cod Hole on the Great Barrier Reef, Queensland. However they are also very common on the closer-inshore Ningaloo Reef off Cape Range in Western Australia, where they may be seen on the outer reef, less than one kilometre from shore. Several of these giants are sometimes observed during a single dive in this area, often hiding among shoals of juvenile fish, parting the shoal in a fan of glittering motion as they cruise through.

Having so few predators, the Potato Cod can afford to be a conspicuous and curious animal. It is fascinated by divers, their bubbles and camera equipment. Tempting these cod with bait is not necessary to attract them, as most will approach divers and swim with them, just for fun.

LEFT *A giant Potato Cod hovers beneath a dive boat, almost certainly waiting for a handout of food.*
BELOW *A dive guide feeding Potato Cod and Red Snappers at Cod Hole on the Great Barrier Reef, Australia.*

CLOSE ENCOUNTERS OF THE COD KIND

Sixty kilograms [132 lb] of Potato Cod swam up to me with its mouth open. Tiny needle-sharp teeth glinted around the periphery of the mouth and I envisaged my whole arm going down its enormous throat. I have seen this happen to others, but usually only when a dead fish is attached to the arm! In this case, perhaps he was yawning, exercising his jaw, or taking a gulp of water. Whatever, he certainly wasn't interested in my arm. He looked at my strobe (flash gun) and decided that it, too, was inedible. He then passed within centimetres of me and continued swimming around the rest of the dive group. This popular animal was probably just looking for a free handout of food, but that is when they can become very aggressive.

My first encounter with a Potato Cod occurred about 16 years ago when a group of us were feeding some of them. One person nearly lost a hand as the cod took the bait-bag, plus the arm, in one bite. Luckily, it let go of the hand and later spat out the bag, minus the fish. On the same dive, my husband thought a practical joker had taken hold of his ankle. As he turned, an enormous cod let him go, but left its mark of tiny teeth in a circle on his skin – through his bootee! Divers have also been bumped during cod feeding frenzies, and several gauges, fins and other apparel have been shaken and torn.

There is nothing more exhilarating and beautiful than coming face to face with a huge, spotted, thick-lipped, adorable Potato Cod. At Ningaloo Reef one or two cod sometimes follow you around for the entire dive, or can be seen in caves and on ledges on the outer reef, where thousands of juvenile fish, often called bait-fish, form thick, swirling, shimmering schools.

Ann Storrie, author of The Marine Life of Ningaloo Marine Park.

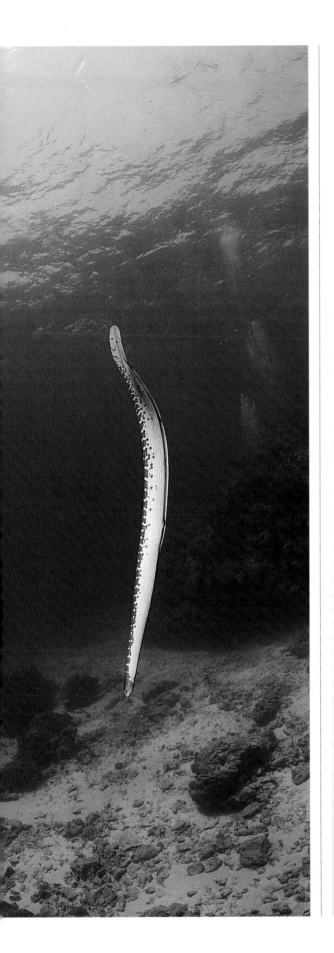

DANCING WITH SEA SNAKES

Jenny screamed, you could hear it clearly underwater. The large Olive Sea Snake looked into her face mask, gave a flick of its tongue and immediately dived straight toward the next terrified onlooker, my husband. He did a delicate pirouette, danced on the spot, then back-pedalled as fast as possible with the snake winding between his legs. In the sidelines, I nearly flooded my mask while choking with laughter. Then the snake headed towards me. I stayed still and waited for it to taste my apparel. It did so with its tongue flicking quickly in and out over my wetsuit, contents gauge and then my face mask. I carefully ran my hand down its streamlined, smooth body. We were friends for life!

I have always loved reptiles, and despite my husband's fear of sea snakes, we have made several trips to the sea snake capital of the world – Western Australia's northern atolls. Twelve of the world's species of sea snakes occur in the area from Scott Reef to Ashmore Reef on the northwest tip of Western Australia. Three of these 12 species occur nowhere other than at Ashmore Reef, and this atoll is the most densely populated area in the world for sea snakes. If one tries, one can find 20 or more snakes on each dive.

Once, on a drift dive, an Olive Sea Snake followed me for 30 minutes. It would stop to poke into crevices in the reef to look for food, then reappear, flick out its tongue, and swim straight towards me. After tasting my fins, it would swim with me for a while before checking the reef again. This cycle continued until the snake surfaced for air.

Since these snakes are some of the most venomous creatures on earth, and many species are not as placid as the Olive Sea Snake, I don't recommend that inexperienced snake handlers touch sea snakes. (Not that that is usually a problem for most divers!)

Sea snakes mating and courting should be given a wide berth, and never try to fend off a sea snake by kicking or pushing it away. An aggressive sea snake can be as terrifying and as deadly as a shark. If a sea snake approaches you, stay still, offer it a fin or camera to taste and it will then usually ignore you.

If you find yourself wrapped in reptiles, swim with them, watch them gracefully glide over the reef, respect them, and remember that it is their domain. You are the intruder.

Ann Storrie, animal technologist, diver and underwater photojournalist.
Wembly, Western Australia.

OPPOSITE *A diver caresses an Olive (Golden) Sea Snake. Only people who are experienced with these snakes should attempt this.*
LEFT *Although very curious of divers, Olive Sea Snakes are rarely aggressive.*

DIVING
IN STRONG
CURRENTS

DIVING IN STRONG CURRENTS IS ESSENTIALLY high-voltage drift-diving. Divers are swept along walls and gullies with the probability of encountering large pelagic species. Apart from the possibility of physical damage if the divers collide with anything, the main problems experienced are those of satisfactory boat cover and becoming separated from one's buddies.

Actual collisions are rare, as the water flow usually sweeps around the object, taking the divers with it. Boat cover is frequently a problem, so divers should use surface marker buoys (SMBs) – highly visible surface floats, sometimes incorporating a dive flag, that are towed along by the diver. SMBs let the surface boat cover know where the divers are and the boat crew can communicate with the divers by jerking the SMB sharply if required.

Only one diver of a buddy pair or group diving together should display an SMB as the lines are easily entangled if several are used close together. They can also cause too much drag if the divers are deep. For this reason each individual diver should carry a delayed deployment SMB that can be released either when the divers are decompressing in shallow water or when they reach the surface. It is also important that each diver has one in case he or she becomes separated from the others.

Delayed deployment SMBs may take the form of collapsible flags or 'rescue sausages' – orange or yellow tubes about 1.5m (5ft) long that are closed at the top end and are open at the base for inflation either by the regulator second stage or via an oral inflation valve. Both types can be raised above the swell to be more visible to the boat cover. Power horns or whistles are better than manual whistles for attracting the attention of the boat cover, but divers should hold them well clear of their ears when in use as they emit a very loud whistle. It is a good idea to ban any form of music on the boat cover, as boat crews will not hear whistles over the sound of loud music.

Dive buddies, and preferably the whole group, should enter the water together so that they do not get separated on the surface and should try to keep together underwater. Stopping to inspect or photograph something will soon separate those concerned from the rest of the group, so it is sensible for photographers to operate in pairs. If divers do get separated from their boat cover, it is wise for them to tie a buddy line between each other, inflate their BCDs and conserve air in case they subsequently have to make a difficult exit through surf or foaming breakers. If divers wish to try finning ashore and are wearing normal BCDs rather than wing BCDs, it is usually less tiring to fin on one's back. At the shore, untie the buddy lines before trying to swim through surf or breakers.

Every diver's worst nightmare is floating on the surface in heavy seas with the surface cover a long way off or completely out of sight. Divers can carry waterproof flares or dye markers that colour the water over a large-enough area to be seen from search aircraft. If you are diving in a country where air search is possible, there are waterproof emergency radio beacons similar to those used by yachtsmen. It is important that divers in this predicament remain tied together.

DIVING
IN STRONG
CURRENTS

PREVIOUS PAGES *Strong currents that sweep around reefs produce high-voltage, high-adrenaline dives that challenge and enthrall even the most experienced divers.*

OPPOSITE *Stopping to inspect or photograph an interesting feature can result in a diver becoming separated from his or her buddy and the entire dive group.*

ABOVE *Anthias and Tubastrea coral at Pelelui Wall, Palau.*

ABOVE RIGHT *A delayed release surface marker buoy is used to indicate the position of a diver completing a decompression stop in the Sudanese Red Sea.*

RIGHT *Currents that are visible on the surface may indicate dangerous underwater conditions, making swimming difficult.*

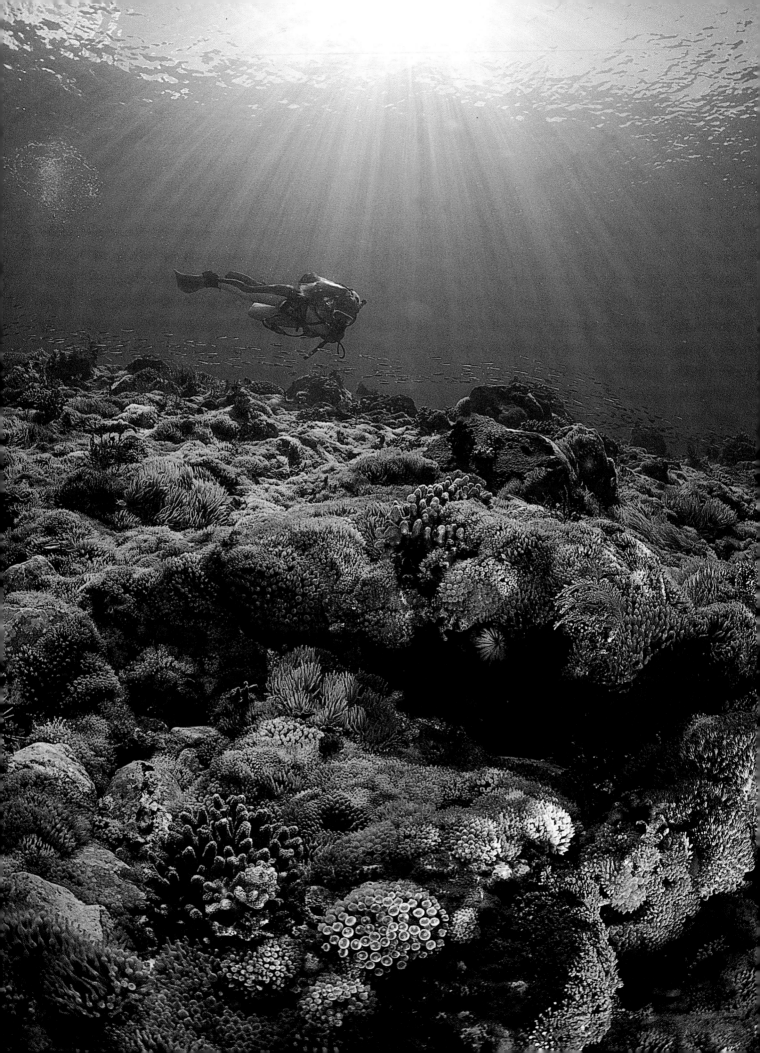

The Canyons, Puerto Galera, Philippines

Diving in the Philippines is known for its currents. There are plenty of sheltered dive sites but in many places the tides sweep across vast areas of the Pacific Ocean with no land mass in the way to slow them down before eddying around the islands. Puerto Galera is at the northern end of the large island of Mindoro Occidental, three hours by road and ferry south of Manila. At the dive site called The Canyons, divers require a knowledgeable local dive guide to show them where to enter the water to allow the currents to carry them to the correct spots, since once in the current, they are committed. Starting on a flood tide just west of Puerto Galera's Escarceo Point, they drop into 9m (30ft) of water, with fields of acropora table corals, and race over several stepped drop-offs to reach The Hole In The Wall. This small hole, covered in multicoloured soft corals, sponges and crinoids, and home to frogfish, scorpionfish, lionfish and trumpetfish, leads to The Canyons. Carried on by the current past an area teeming with fish, divers sweep around Escarceo Point into a bowl-shaped depression at 40m (130ft) known as The Fish Bowl, where they look down at an abundance of shoaling fish and their predators. Whitetip Reef Sharks, Grey Reef Sharks, large tuna, shoals of Rainbow Runners, batfish, snappers, Oriental Sweetlips, Spotted Sweetlips, fusiliers, jacks and Barracuda as well as lone groupers, trigger-fish, surgeonfish, filefish and giant trevally mill around. Manta Rays, lone Thresher Sharks and, in the winter, large Hammerhead Sharks have also been seen, so divers should look up as well as down.

Dragged on by the current, the divers fight their way into the shelter of some large rocks, check out several moray eels and octopuses and then move around the corner where the current picks them up again and sweeps them into the canyons, which can be used to shelter from the current. The first canyon drops to 26m (85ft); the second, reaching to 28m (92ft), has great Gorgonian Sea Fans; while the third is deeper and often has a shoal of snappers using it for shelter. After the third canyon, the coral and fish life gets really prolific again but is exposed to the current. The same species as at the Fish Bowl exist here, with the addition of Six Banded, Royal and Emperor Angelfish, and butterflyfish. The deeper water has large turtles, barrel sponges, Gorgonian Sea Whips and Gorgonian Sea Fans.

If they manage to get the current right, the divers are eventually swept onto an old, large 1.5m (5ft) anchor at 26m (85ft); it may have come from a wreck or simply been abandoned. The divers can hang on to this anchor while the group gathers together again. When they let go they are swept away in the current and ascend slowly to decompress in open water, being careful to keep to the correct depths and inflating a delayed deployment surface marker buoy. As high-voltage dives go, this is one of the best, but be warned, the currents can be fierce at the peak of a flood tide and can be difficult on an ebb tide. Photographers should aim to dive as near as possible to slack water.

Blue Corner, Palau, Micronesia

Anyone who researches Palau (also known as Belau), one of the Caroline Islands in Micronesia, as a dive destination will come across stories of currents 'that almost rip your mask off'. In fact, these currents only occur for brief periods at certain times of the month and are only felt when hanging on to a reef, not when drifting with the currents. In Palau there are generally four tidal changes a day and diving is planned around them. At times of half-moon, reef areas that form a corner have stronger currents and associated fish action; at full or new moon the stronger currents occur in the channels. Currents will be strongest at times of spring tides and weakest at times of neap tides.

At Blue Corner, the currents may be so strong that divers can be swept off the reef. Some divers overcome this by using a reef hook – a small, heavy, shark-fishing hook with the barb filed off and the tip filed blunt. One end of the hook is attached to a short, strong line and the other end to a karabiner (snaplink). It is then hooked into a nook or cranny among a patch of dead coral on the reef and the karabiner is clipped to the diver's BCD. Some air is then added to the BCD to keep the diver clear of the reef and he or she faces into the current. (If divers turn their heads away from the current it can feel

OPPOSITE Strong currents sweep a diver across the reef.
TOP Blackfin Barracuda shoal at Blue Corner, Palau
BELOW Yellow Wall, Palau is another dive that can have strong currents.

ABOVE *The Arch, an aptly named rock formation on Palau.*
BELOW *A diver comes face to face with a Giant Humphead (Napoleon) Wrasse at Palau's Blue Corner.*

as though the mask and regulator are about to be ripped from their faces.) Once attached in this way, divers can relax, catch their breath, let their heartbeat return to normal, comfortably check instruments and watch the fish action. Of course reef hooks will damage the coral (see panel opposite), but they are only used in certain areas when strong currents are running and divers must pause to watch the action. The majority of Palau's currents are manageable, so reef hooks are not required, but where they are, most operators issue them.

Blue Corner faces toward the Philippine Sea. When flood tides come up against the wall, nutrient-rich water is forced upward providing food that attracts smaller fish, which in turn attract larger predators. To start the dive, divers dodge the worst of the current by quickly descending 30m (100ft) to gain shelter from a wall that drops to over 300m (1000ft). They then swim in the current to the reef's western edge. Shortly before a sharp bend in the wall called The Corner, there is an indent which, in strong currents, can feature an upwelling referred to as The Elevator. If divers get caught in this upwelling, there is little chance of them being able to get their reef hooks attached on top of the reef.

Off the wall, Blacktip, Grey Reef and Whitetip Reef Sharks charge into shoals of barracuda, surgeonfish, snappers and jacks, picking off their prey. When the dive guide finds the correct place, the divers rise to the top of the wall where they have about five seconds to find an area of dead coral to hook onto, otherwise the current sweeps them off the reef and they miss the fish action. Once safely attached, divers can watch the sharks. Napoleon Wrasse approach closely and the reef top harbours Redtooth Triggerfish, Moorish Idols, fusiliers, turtles, angelfish and butterflyfish.

Many divers are soon low on air, so the dive guide signals all the divers to unhook at the same time. Swept off the reef they slowly ascend to 5m (16ft) for a safety stop where the dive guide deploys a SMB to alert the boat cover, and spell the end of an electrifying dive.

Cocos Island, off Costa Rica

In strong currents, diving conditions are not predictable, and while divers are rewarded with big animal encounters, dealing with the currents often takes precedence. One must react quickly, decreasing buoyancy when caught in an upwelling, or increasing it when caught in a downwelling. Divers are sometimes able to escape an upwelling by swimming away from the reef and a downwelling by swimming closer to the reef. Contrary to many sensational reports, most downwelling currents occur at walls and dissipate before reaching extreme depths. Remember that whatever countermeasures have been taken in an up- or downwelling, they must immediately be reversed to re-establish neutral buoyancy when divers are no longer in that particular current. Keep an eye on the bubbles of the divers ahead. If they begin descending or moving in circles, the divers are experiencing a downwelling or washing machine-type current which can then either be avoided or planned for.

At Cocos Island, off the Pacific coast of Costa Rica, strong currents are present at many sites, particularly those with exciting action such as Dirty Rock or Manuelita and much of the action is out in open water. Currents will be strongest at times of spring tide and weakest at times of neap tide.

The entire dive group should enter the water together and descend as quickly as possible to avoid the surface chop and current. At depths between 18 and 30m (60 and 100ft) each buddy pair should look for shelter among large boulders, hanging on if necessary, as there is no coral to kill. The first thing divers will notice is the sheer abundance of Whitetip Reef Sharks as they descend on large

ABOVE *A surface marker buoy (SMB) being deployed underwater. In strong currents, these alert the boat cover to the diver's position at the end of the dive.*
LEFT *Conscientiously placed reef hooks enable the diver to stay off the coral while maintaining a position in the current.*

REEF HOOKS – GOOD OR BAD?

Diving Palau's Blue Corner is never easy, even for strong swimmers. It helps if divers are fit, correctly weighted and able to descend quickly, as on top of the wall they are easily swept away by the current. This is why reef hooks were invented here. Once hooked into dead coral, divers face the current, become human kites and relax to watch the fish action. The experts hook in quickly and efficiently with little damage, but novices often scrabble around, killing coral as they try to attach themselves. Divers hooked in do far less damage than if they were holding onto the reef, but large areas of the coral are now dead. Conservation-minded divers argue against the practice but the site is so popular that the use of reef hooks is unlikely to be banned. It would be worth installing fixed hooking points along the reef to which divers could attach themselves, keeping coral damage to a minimum.

packs of them, often piled one on top of the other, resting on the sand. Out at the limits of visibility, males are often engaged in a mating ritual with a female, biting her as they circle her.

Divers commonly encounter bait-balls (shoals of jacks so dense that they can block out the sun), snappers, lone groupers, pufferfish, Moray Eels, trumpetfish, frogfish, and the occasional Red-lip Batfish, together with Green and Hawksbill Turtles, lobsters and octopuses. Any crevices in the reef are packed with fish hiding from the current and predators, but most divers do not endure the long boat trip out from the mainland to see the smaller animals. Divers soon ignore the ever-present Whitetip Reef Sharks and search out the unmistakable shape of Hammerhead Sharks. Sometimes these sharks are encountered near to the surface but mostly they are found below the thermoclines. Most of the diving is between 18 and 30m (60 and 100ft), occasionally reaching down to 40m (130ft). Squadrons of Scalloped Hammerhead Sharks appear out of the blue, swim majestically by and recede into the distance, only to be replaced by further shoals, numbering 10, 20, 50, even hundreds of animals at a time.

Adding to the excitement are encounters with Manta Rays, shoaling Mobula and Eagle Rays, Silky Sharks, Galapagos Sharks and occasionally, dolphins or a Whale Shark. The Mobula Rays often approach divers, looking to have their bodies rubbed as if by cleaner fish.

Depending on the strength of the current, at a prearranged scuba cylinder air pressure the divers will move out from behind the protective boulders and let the current carry them away while slowly ascending to the depth of a safety stop. The stronger the current the earlier they should rise, at half air pressure if it is really strong. At Manuelita, the divers can let the current carry them to the calmer leeward side of the islet but wherever they are they would perform a safety stop at around 5m (16ft), deploy a safety sausage SMB and surface to be picked up by the boat cover.

Reefs on drop-offs are inhabited by a variety of shoaling fish, including Black Snappers (BELOW) and Big-eye Trevallies (BOTTOM), which are found at many sites in the Pacific Ocean.

Cozumel, Yucatán Peninsula, Mexico

The small island of Cozumel, which lies some 30km (20 miles) off the coast of Mexico's Yucatán Peninsula, is regarded as one of the world's top drift-diving destinations. It is located at the northern end of a barrier reef that stretches from southern Belize, spanning nearly 245km (150 miles), making it the second longest barrier reef in the sea. Situated where the Caribbean Current – part of the North Equatorial Current that runs clockwise around the outer edges of the Caribbean Sea – squeezes between Mexico and the southern tip of Cuba, Cozumel lies in a moving river of ocean, driven by the trade winds. A strong northward current is the norm.

The constantly flowing water feeds an extremely healthy and dynamic reef system. Especially along the southwestern coast and extending off the island's southern tip, a coral-covered wall drops steeply away to very deep water. Only 12m (40ft) deep in most areas, the wall edge is a jumble of large coral mounds, grottoes, overhangs and sheer faces. Due to a strong conservation programme, there are many fish, especially large snappers, groupers, barracuda and many colourful reef fish such as angelfish and butterflyfish. With the constantly flowing water, which usually runs at least 1.85km (one knot) per hour, the visibility is normally excellent, often reaching over 38m (125ft).

Diving Cozumel's reefs requires care, and a knowledgeable local guide is normally considered essential. The current is generally too strong to dive from an anchored boat and chase-boats are necessary to dive the most desirable areas. While there are many diving areas around the small island, the most popular is the Palancar Reef region, located along the southern shoreline, on the western side. Beginning with a shallow sandy bottom, the reef drops away steeply to very deep water. Along the edge, large growths of corals, sponges and Gorgonian Sea Fans create a fairyland of colour and strange shapes. At some places, the wall is steep and smooth; at others, there are

canyons and sand-chutes that begin well back from the wall, then run toward it until they spill dizzily over the edge. The current is usually so strong on Palancar that an hour's exciting dive may carry divers for more than 1.5km (1 mile), soaring effortlessly over the living reef.

Just to the north of Palancar, Santa Rosa Reef is considered one of Cozumel's prettiest diving areas. A brilliant white sand bottom, just a few hundred metres offshore, is covered with large coral structures along the top of a slope where the water deepens. The rapidly flowing current has allowed the coral to form intricate mazes and twisted patterns. Tunnels, grottoes and shallow caverns, covered with colourful growths of sponges and encrusting corals, provide divers with momentary respites from the rapidly moving water, which in its main flow is usually too strong to allow stopping for more than a moment.

Off the southern tip of the island, in an area called Maracaibo Reef, Cozumel's more exciting drift dives are reserved for advanced divers. The reef here is deeper, with most dives reaching at least 25–30m (80–100ft). Because the area is away from the wind protection of the shoreline, there may also be surface swell and chop in addition to the swift current. Divers must take care to stay together, otherwise they can become scattered over a wide area of open ocean during the course of a dive and as a result, be difficult to find at the end of the dive. For those qualified to dive the Caribbean's Maracaibo Reef, it is among the best of high-voltage diving. The bottom is a constantly changing jumble of coral spires and boulders with a steeply inclined wall. Big fish are commonplace, among them the metre-long Black Groupers and 75cm (30in) Mutton Snappers, which feed along the drop-offs. The heady combination of strong currents, depth and big animals makes for thrilling diving.

Above Palancar Reef, off Cozumel is home to many large corals, sponges and Gorgonian Sea Fans, as well as several fish species. The current is fast and the visibility excellent, making for an exhilarating dive.

WRECK
DIVING

SHIPWRECKS ARE THE MOST POPULAR DIVE SITES in temperate, low-visibility waters, while in warmer waters they harbour prolific coral and sponge growth. In both areas they are a haven of fish life. Wrecks occur for many reasons, including armed conflicts, bad weather, careless navigation and insurance fraud. Environmentally cleaned wrecks are also sunk specifically for diving.

Some divers spend their lives researching archives for clues to a wreck's location or history, either out of historical and archaeological interest or with monetary gain in mind through salvage or treasure. Most divers simply enjoy diving wrecks, but some cause problems for those who follow by desecrating war graves or the wrecks of civilian disasters, or removing artefacts and denying later divers the pleasure of seeing them, while also incurring the wrath of archaeologists and governments.

Diving around the exterior of shallow wrecks does not require special skills. In a current, divers must quickly descend the shotline to reach the lee of the wreck; in bad visibility they may have to use compass bearings from the bottom of the shotline. One extra problem is that most wrecks are snagged with fishing nets and lines.

Penetrating easy wrecks is not difficult. One should choose slack water, carry a good light, a backup light and a sharp implement for cutting monofilament fishing line or nets. Dive-knives strapped to legs can be dislodged by lifelines or tangled in fishing lines or nets, so carry a separate smaller knife attached to one arm, or cut-through-anything shears in the BCD pocket, where they are easily reached.

The first pair of divers onto the wreck should tie a shotline off to the wreck, and the final pair of divers to ascend should release it. Secure all of your equipment against your body so that it will not snag. To penetrate a wreck that is new to you without a guide, tie off a lifeline before entering and feed it out as you go. This will enable you to retrace your route if you become disoriented when sediment is stirred up. Hands, fins and exhaust bubbles can all disturb sediment. Leave yourself plenty of air to get out again and tie up all doors and hatches that you pass through, so that they cannot close on you in a current.

Penetrating more difficult wrecks requires all the skills of diving in closed overhead environments and deep wrecks require mixed gas technical diving skills.

PREVIOUS PAGES *Wrecks, such as the Giannis D, in the Egyptian Red Sea, offer another dimension to divers who wish to explore a different underwater world.*
ABOVE *A diver attaching a shotline to the Thistlegorm. The shotline assists with ascent and descent, especially in strong currents.*
OPPOSITE TOP *Searching for artefacts is a popular pastime, but local and international laws on shipwrecks and salvage should always be observed.*
OPPOSITE TOP RIGHT *Stern view of the Umbria, Red Sea.*
OPPOSITE BOTTOM RIGHT *A Lionfish rests on a truck in Truk.*

MAXIMUM DEPTH OF FEATURED WRECKS

Rhone	British Virgin Islands	24m	72ft
Yongala	Great Barrier Reef	27m	89ft
Duane	Florida Keys	27m	89ft
Shinkoku	Truk Lagoon, Micronesia	29m	95ft
Fumitsuki	Truk Lagoon, Micronesia	30m	100
Thistlegorm	Egyptian Red Sea	32m	105
Umbria (bow)	Sudanese Red Sea	36m	118
Proteus	North Carolina	39m	125
Bibb	Florida Keys	40m	130
San Francisco	Truk Lagoon, Micronesia	46m	150
Pres. Coolidge (stern)	Vanuatu	70m	230
Andrea Doria	Nantucket	73m	240
Lusitania	Ireland	93m	305
Britannic	Athens	120m	394

WRECK DIVING

WRECKS AND THE LAW

Most countries have different and often-confusing laws regarding diving wrecks. Many Third World governments have none at all on the subject and others, despite giving permission for salvage, often renege on agreements and confiscate anything valuable found.

The problems are: ownership, archaeological and heritage value, and loss of life. The latter issue is further complicated by often only covering the sanctity of military personnel in declared 'war graves' and not civilian casualties in either wartime or peacetime. Although governments cannot control war graves that are not in their own waters, they have often contradicted themselves by issuing licences for salvors to salvage valuables from a war grave, but then refused to allow divers to dive it. Some countries have proposed laws so draconian that they would stop all wreck diving; others refuse to allow wrecks to be specifically sunk for diving in case they become liable for accidents on them.

Where voluntary restraints exist, divers should obey them to avoid giving bureaucrats the excuse to ban all sport diving on wrecks. Those diving wrecks in their own country should first become thoroughly conversant with the local laws; when diving in foreign countries, local dive operators should understand local regulations.

BELOW *A diver prepares to enter the century-old wreck of the RMS* Rhone. *British Virgin Islands.*
OPPOSITE TOP *Penetration of the Rhone is easy and safe for all divers.*
OPPOSITE BOTTOM *Squirrelfish shelter on the RMS* Rhone.

RMS *Rhone*, British Virgin Islands

One of the first ships to have a metal hull, the Royal Mail Steamship (RMS) *Rhone* was only two years old when she perished in one of the worst storms ever experienced in the Caribbean. Built in London's Millwall Iron Works and launched in February 1865, she was 94m (310ft) long with a 12m (40ft) beam and a displacement of 2416 tonnes. Powered by both steam and sail she carried mail, passengers and general cargo to South America via St Thomas in the US Virgin Islands, where she refuelled with coal.

In the mid-1800s an outbreak of yellow fever in St Thomas caused ships to use the smaller port of Road Harbour at Road Town, capital of Tortola in the British Virgin Islands. At 11:00 on 2 October 1867, RMS *Rhone* was anchored off Peter Island, just across the main channel from Road Town, when a hurricane struck. During a lull in the storm, Captain Wooley tried to weigh anchor but the 1360kg (3000 lb) anchor snagged and was lost with 91m (300ft) of chain.

Finally the *Rhone* managed to steam out to sea, but the wind changed direction and forced her, stern first, onto Black Rock Point, the westernmost end of Salt Island. The superheated boilers exploded on contact with the cooler sea water, killing passengers and breaking the ship in two. Early divers using primitive equipment managed to salvage the £60,000 in bullion, but 123 out of the 145 passengers and crew died.

The ferocity of the hurricane wreaked havoc. As well as the damage on land, The Royal Mail Steam Packet Company lost three ships – the *Rhone*, the *Derwent* and the *Wye* – and two others, the *Solent* and the *Tyne,* were badly damaged. Over 60 vessels and 500 lives were lost.

Today this twin-masted steamer lies where she sank, the 1998 hurricane George having only moved her scattered debris around a bit. She is in distinct sections from 9–24m (30–79ft) deep, with her stern and single 6m (19ft) propeller in the shallower water. There are several mooring buoys but sometimes the currents are so strong that diving is not sensible.

Divers often treat the ship as two distinct dives, for safety, beginning with the deeper bow section first and then working back towards the shallows.

Lying on its starboard side, the bow section is almost intact, the traditional bowsprit eliciting memories of 'tall ships'. The wooden decking has rotted away, while its column-like supporting girders and the foremast with its crow's-nest, encrusted with marine growth, are popular areas for divers and underwater photography. The mid-sec-

tion has the remains of the boilers, one still attached to the mid-section while the other is lying near the stern. The exploded boilers have left a large opening, making it easy for divers to penetrate the hollow bow section so long as they have good buoyancy control. Inside the bow section, there is prolific marine life with shoals of Bluestriped Grunts, goatfish, Blackbar Soldierfish and lone Barracuda. This cave-like area is dark, there is even black coral found here, but a safe exit is always visible.

From the rear boiler to the stern, the wreckage is more difficult to identify until one reaches the propeller shaft and the massive propeller. Necks of champagne bottles protrude from solid marine growth of stony corals, fire coral and sponges.

In 1976 the RMS *Rhone* was used as a film set for Steven Spielberg's Hollywood blockbuster *The Deep*, based on Peter Benchley's book of the same name. It is now the most popular wreck in the Caribbean, so divers need to get there very early to avoid the crowds.

Truk Lagoon, Chuuk, Micronesia

Perhaps the world's most impressive wreck diving is found in Truk Lagoon among the islands of Chuuk, a collection of jungled mountaintops thrusting up from the bottom of a huge, reef-encircled lagoon in the western Pacific, east of the Caroline Islands.

When World War II began, the Japanese military turned this quiet archipelago into a naval fortress, second in size only to the US base at Pearl Harbour, Hawaii. Truk Lagoon was the staging point for numerous Japanese war campaigns and was a crucial link in the supply line to support Japanese forces throughout the region. It was estimated that 60 attack submarines, 250 merchant ships and 125 warships, operated out of Truk, supported by fuel depots, dry docks, airfields, communications centres, and 40,000 Japanese soldiers.

ABOVE *Truk Lagoon, Chuuk.*
BELOW LEFT *Diver examining a bulldozer on the wreck of the* Hoki Maru, *originally the confiscated British freighter* MV Hauraki.
BELOW CENTRE *A plaque on the* Fujikawa Maru *commemorating the 50th anniversary of Operation Hailstorm.*
BELOW RIGHT Sankisan Maru, *showing the hold full of bullets. The original wooden boxes have rotted away.*

As the American military began its move to recapture the Pacific, the lagoon became a key target, and rather than invade, the American forces decided to bomb the islands into submission. In a series of air attacks, beginning with Operation Hailstorm in February 1944, the USA completely demolished the islands' fortifications, sank some 80 ships and destroyed nearly 450 aircraft.

When the war ended, Chuuk again became merely a quiet, remote group of islands, far off the beaten track and largely forgotten by the outside world. Mother Nature reclaimed the islands and covered the destruction of war, both in the jungles and under the calm surface of the lagoon.

Today, on the bottom of Truk Lagoon are the remains of more than 70 Japanese ships enshrouded by an unimaginably brilliant covering of soft corals, sponges and shellfish, and attracting swirling shoals of fish. Each wreck, still filled with its original cargo and the personal effects of its crew, has been transformed into an artificial reef of immense proportions.

Divers can visit as many as four different shipwrecks in a day, each one unique. A visit to Truk Lagoon is a varied experience due to the splendour of the natural environment, the awesome size and mystery of huge warships lying quietly on the bottom, and a pervading, thought-provoking sense of history.

Among the interesting wrecks is the destroyer *Fumitsuki*. Nearly 90m (300ft) long, she lies upright in 30m (100ft) of warm, clear water. Bristling with torpedo tubes, guns and depth charge launchers, her stern guns point aft and the personal belongings of her crew – shoes, sake bottles, gramophone records and books – are scattered about the deck. The ship's once clean lines are softened by a draping of soft corals, and a resident school of friendly batfish swims lazily about.

Another incredible ship is the *Shinkoku Maru,* a 152m-long (500ft) tanker that has become a gigantic garden of colour. In 29m (95ft) of water, with her wheelhouse at only 14m (45ft), her masts, rigging and decks are enveloped in soft corals and anemones, whose barrel-shaped bodies glow in amazing shades of pink, blue, emerald and orange. The ship's telegraph is still reading full speed ahead.

For those qualified to visit deeper wrecks, there is the *San Francisco* with her main deck at 46m (150ft). Her hold is full of mines, bombs and other ordinance and the large forecastle gun is amazingly well-preserved. Her deck cargo of three armoured tanks and a truck still quietly wait for their mission.

With these and so many more ships to dive, Truk Lagoon can be visited over and over again without ever seeing everything. As time goes by, the marine growth on the ships continues to accumulate, while the island government's protectionist policy over its sunken graveyard ensures that Truk Lagoon will remain a marvel for divers for many years to come.

ABOVE *Divers on the popular wreck of the* Fujikawa Maru *in Truk Lagoon.*
BELOW LEFT *Soft Tree Corals are a colourful sight on the* Kansho Maru.
BELOW RIGHT *The coral encrusted* Shinkoku Maru.

ABOVE *Divers exit the Black Island Wreck in Coron Bay,*
Palawan, Philippines
BELOW *Blast damage on the main deck of the Japanese*
freighter Olympia Maru *in Coron Bay, Philippines.*

Coron and Busuanga Islands, Philippines

In 1944, US Admiral 'Bull' Halsey ordered reconnaissance aircraft to photograph the Linapacan Strait, which leads into the South China Sea south–southwest of Manila, to survey the Japanese firepower in preparation for the American landing on Leyte and the Calamian islands. When an observant mapping officer noticed that some of the islands could move, the Americans realized that they had found a camouflaged Japanese fleet. At 09:00 hours on 24 September, carrier-based Grumman Hellcat and Helldiver aircraft attacked and sank at least 18 vessels around Busuanga Island. Today, 14 of these wrecks have been located and, together with a wooden fishing boat, have become havens for wreck fanatics.

Off the beach on the east side of Malajon Island, the Black Island Wreck, a 45m (150ft) coastal vessel of unknown origin sits upright, tilted down the sandy slope with the bow at 32m (105ft) and the stern at 20m (65ft). South of Concepçion village, the 10,206-tonne, 168m-long (550ft) oil tanker *Taiei Maru* (also known as Concepçion Wreck) lies listing slightly to port with the main deck at 16m (52ft) and the bow broken off at 26m (85ft). Between Lajo and Manglet Islands, the 4724-tonne 148m-long (486ft) flying-boat tender *Akitsushima*, rests on her port side in 38m (125ft) of water. The arm of the stern crane, used to load and unload the flying-boat, lies broken to port at 34m (112ft). The main deck is split between this crane and the funnel. A salvaged gunboat lies from the surface to 10m (33ft) at the southern end of Lusong Island, while between the northern ends of Lusong and Tangat islands, a 5707-tonne, 137m (449ft) long freighter, believed to be the *Olympia Maru*, lies on her starboard side in 25m (80ft) of water.

South of the *Olympia Maru,* east of the southeast corner of Lusong Island, the 6454-tonne 158m-long (518ft).freighter *Kogyo Maru* lies on her starboard side in 34m (112ft) of water.

South of the *Kogyo Maru,* southeast of Lusong island, the 9723-tonne, 147m-long (482ft) refrigerated provision ship *Irako* lists 10 degrees to port in 42m (138ft) of water. Penetration of this vessel is an advanced dive due to the depth, but the superstructure is interesting.

West of the southwest end of Tangat Island lies Tangat Wreck. There is much dispute over this wreck. Some researchers think that this is in fact the real *Olympia Maru,* while others think it is a British combined cargo and passenger vessel named *SS Manco,* she was later renamed *SS Morazon* after being seized by the Japanese and later renamed *Ekkai Maru.* This easily penetrated 3190-tonne, 92m-long (300ft) wreck lists 15 degrees to port in 30m (100ft) of water.

Southeast of Tangat Island, the 508-tonne East Tangat Wreck is believed to be either a tugboat or anti-submarine craft. Measuring 40m (130ft) in length, she lies listing to starboard down a sandy slope with the stern at 22m (72ft) and the top of the bow at 3m (10ft). A small wreck that has been salvaged, she is mostly shallow enough for snorkelling.

North of Busuanga Island, lies the 6596-tonne, 152m-long (499ft) freighter *Kyokuzan Maru,* listing 15 degrees to starboard in 43m (141ft) of water. Almost intact, the main deck slopes from 22–28m (72–92ft) and the easily penetrated holds contain the remains of her cargo of cars and trucks. This wreck is very close to Dimilanta Island, so it is always well protected from the weather. Although a lot of the cargo and some engines have been salvaged, the whole area resembles a miniature Truk Lagoon.

ABOVE *Superstructure of the Shallow Water Wreck off Coron Island showing Alabaster Sea Cucumbers and sponges.*
BELOW *The corroded hull and ribs of a Gun Boat, possibly a U-boat hunter, at Tangat Island, Coron.*

The *Umbria*, Sudanese Red Sea

If ever a wreck was designed to please recreational divers, it is the *Umbria*. Scuttled in shallow water off Port Sudan, in the Red Sea, and sheltered by Wingate Reefs she can be dived in any weather. There is no current, lots of light, great visibility, abundant coral growth and prolific marine life.

Originally named *Bahia Blanca*, this 10,237-tonne 155m-long (509ft) combined cargo and passenger vessel was built in Hamburg in 1912. Before World War II she was sold to Lloyd Triestino Di Navigazione Societa Per Azioni, renamed *Umbria* and registered at Genoa. She was anchored outside Port Sudan harbour on 12 June 1940, when Italy entered the war in support of Germany. Knowing that it carried munitions, and vehicle and aircraft spares hidden under cement and foodstuffs, the British authorities seized the ship; but the crew had opened the seacocks and the captain lied that timed fuses had been set in the munitions holds. The ship was abandoned to sink.

Considered a danger to shipping movements in the anchorage, a Royal Navy survey judged the munitions unstable from exposure to sea water and predicted that if they were to explode, the concave reef behind the *Umbria* would reflect a tidal wave into the main harbour, causing considerable damage. It was decided to mark the vessel on the charts as dangerous, and the area around it was forbidden to shipping.

In 1949, defying local thinking that sharks would attack him, pioneering diver Hans Hass became the first civilian brave enough to dive on the *Umbria*. His book *Under the Red Sea*, first published in 1952, and his subsequent films, attracted the world's top underwater photographers to the site. Today the *Umbria* lies at an angle on her port side, with her starboard davits breaking the surface. The port propeller is buried in the coral, but the starboard propeller is in clear water at 15m (50ft). The stern rests on coral at 20m (65ft), while the bow rests at 36m (118ft).

The *Umbria* is visited by a variety of species. Manta Rays, turtles and dolphins pass by, small Whitetip Reef Sharks often hide under the stern in a cave between the propellers, and Spanish Dancers and Spiny Lobsters are seen on night dives.

Penetrating most of the ship is easy. The gangways are clear and the holds are open with ammunition shells, bullets, bombs, fuses, aircraft and vehicle parts, wine bottles, batteries and glass jars scattered around. Many sacks are no longer supported so divers require good buoyancy control to avoid dislodging them. Entering the engine room and kitchen are more difficult. Divers must be careful not to disturb the silt or they will not be able to see their way out again. A fixed safety guideline is a prudent precaution here. The engines are still intact and an outboard motor is still clamped to the engine room wall. Crockery with the Lloyd Triestino emblem can still be found in the kitchen.

The *Umbria* is one of the world's greatest dives and one of the most photogenic wrecks, and it is not surprising that it is often used as a set for feature films.

BELOW *The well-lit companionway of the wreck of the* Umbria, *scuttled inside Wingate Reef, Port Sudan, Red Sea.*

ABOVE LEFT A Crown of Thorns Sea Star and two Threadfin Butterflyfish feed on 40 years of coral growth on the Umbria.
ABOVE RIGHT By returning regularly to the same wreck, divers can track the growth of corals and the proliferation of marine life. These Yellowbar (Half Moon) Angelfish were photographed on the Umbria nearly 50 years after she sank.
BELOW In April 1980, after an interval of more than 30 years, Hans Hass returned to the Umbria.

DIVING WITH HANS HASS

The father of modern underwater photography, Hans Hass wrote his first book about hunting with cameras in 1939 and, together with the German company Franke & Heidecke, developed the Rolleimarine underwater housing for the Twin-Lens Rolleiflex Camera in 1949.

Despite local warnings about sharks, Hass was the first civilian to dive the *Umbria,* in 1949. His books and television films did much to popularize scuba diving in Europe in the 1950s and 1960s. He retired from scientific diving in 1962 to focus on research into human evolution, but he continued to make underwater films. In 1980, 30 years after he first filmed the *Umbria,* Hass returned to the Red Sea to film and photograph the wreck again in order to find out how much it had changed. He asked me to join him as safety diver. Working with the old maestro was an experience in itself. We spent four days diving around the wreck with black and white prints of his original photographs in our hands. They were not exactly waterproof, but the images lasted long enough for us to look for any areas we recognized, so that Hass could rephotograph them. Most of the brass portholes and steam valves had not yet been removed, but the funnel and mast had collapsed since his first visit, when these both broke the surface. The coral growth and fish life that the *Umbria* had attracted in the intervening years were prolific.

Business on the *Umbria* over, we finished the week with a long, deep dive to view the Hammerhead Sharks of Sanganeb's North Point. Hass was a heavy breather, so I carried an extra scuba cylinder of air fitted with a regulator for him to use – otherwise this was just another dive for the then 62-year-old adventurer!

Jack Jackson is an Advanced BS-AC diver, who ran a sport diving operation and a diving boat in the Sudanese Red Sea for 12 years.

SS Thistlegorm, Egypt

One of the Red Sea's most popular wrecks, the 4976 tonne, 126.5m-long (415ft), 365-horsepower, triple-expansion-engined *SS Thistlegorm* was built by JL Thompson and Sons at Sunderland in 1940. Requisitioned and armed by the navy she set off with supplies for the British 8th Army at Alexandria in North Africa. The Germans and Italians had control of the Mediterranean, so she sailed the long route, around the Cape of Good Hope and was escorted up the Red Sea to Suez. Laden with military equipment – from vehicle and aircraft parts, motorcycles, gun carriers, munitions and two railway loco-motives to radios and Wellington boots (gumboots) – she was held up with other ships at Sha'b Ali as the passage to the Suez Canal was slowed by a stricken vessel called the *Tynefield*.

On 5 October 1941, two German Heinkel HE-111 bombers took off from the Luftwaffe's 26th Bomber Group at Heraklion Airfield in Crete on a mission to find and bomb the *Queen Mary*. Having failed to find her, and running low on fuel, they turned back north and decided to drop their bombs on the first ship they found. At 01:30 on Monday 6 October they found the ships in the anchorage. Both planes dropped a pair of bombs and two of them hit the aft holds of the *Thistlegorm,* one of them directly on number four hold, which contained ordinance. The resulting explosions ripped a huge hole in the aft section, blew a locomotive and its tender off the deck to the port side and set the ship on fire. Nine of the 39 crew were killed. As was the custom at the time, the surviving crew's pay was stopped and they had to make their own way home.

In the years immediately after the war, British ships lowered their ensigns as they passed the spot and the wreck was marked on early postwar charts as a danger to shipping. In the early 1950s it was easy for

BELOW *A diver manages to escape the crowds at the wreck of the* Thistlegorm, *Shag Rock, Sha'b Ali, Egyptian Red Sea.*

Captain Jacques-Yves Cousteau and his crew to find the *Thistlegorm* and salvage some artefacts, including the captain's safe, a BSA motorcycle and the ship's bell. In both his film and book *The Living Sea,* Cousteau called the wreck a 'time capsule'. What is surprising is that since the 1970s, the area was constantly being dived, yet everyone except the local Bedouin fishermen had forgotten about the *Thistlegorm.* In early 1990, divers woke up to the fact that she was out there, began asking questions and rediscovered her. Not as good as the *Umbria,* because the visibility was often poor and the currents strong, in those days she was still reminiscent of a war museum. Tool kits could be found under the seats of the motorcycles. Nurse Sharks and huge groupers rested among the wreckage and the handrails were covered in corals and sponges. Despite attempts to keep the discovery quiet, word soon got out and divers arrived in hordes.

Today the *Thistlegorm* resembles an underwater army surplus store. Situated northeast of Shag Rock, east of the southern end of Sha'b Ali, northwest of Râs Muhammad, she is almost upright, slightly listing to port except for the stern section, which lies heavily to port. The bottom of the bow is at 30m (100ft), the propeller and rudder are at 32m (105ft) and the superstructure rises to 12m (40ft).

Conditions at the site vary, but get there very early to avoid the hordes and she is still a tremendous dive. Wreckers have done their damage, but the holds still contain all the implements of World War II and the marine life is abundant.

Above *A diver is dwarfed by the* Thistlegorm's *propeller. The ship was one of many vessels sunk in the Red Sea by German bombers during World War II.*
Left *Negotiating a ladder on the* Thistlegorm. *Over the years divers have taken pleasure in discovering the wide variety of military equipment she carried − everything from aircraft parts and motorcyles to radios and Wellington boots.*

SS Yongala, Queensland, Australia

Nobody will ever know what caused the demise of the ill-fated 3722-tonne *SS Yongala*. All we know is that she unwittingly sailed into a cyclone and sank in a shipping channel 18km (11 miles) east of Cape Bowling Green between Australia's Queensland coast and the Great Barrier Reef.

Built of steel by Armstrong Whitworth and Company, the opulent steamship *Yongala*, 111m (363ft) long and 14m (45.3ft) wide, began her life at sea on 29 April 1903. Owned and operated by the Adelaide Steamship Company as a combined cargo-passenger vessel, she spent her first three years travelling the south coast of Australia between Sydney and Fremantle. In 1907 she began serving the east coast, between Melbourne in the south and Cairns in the north.

For her 99th and last voyage, she left Melbourne on 14 March 1911 under Captain Knight, carrying passengers, timber, bricks, tyres and foodstuffs. On 23 March, she called at Flat-top Island (the Mackay anchorage prior to the building of an artificial harbour here in 1939), some 640km (400 miles) south of Cairns, where three passengers disembarked and two more embarked. At 13:40 she departed Mackay with 49 passengers, 72 crew and a racehorse called Moonshine, which was due to race in Townsville, 335km (210 miles) away.

She was last seen passing the Dent Island Lighthouse at 19:00 on the 23rd but not having radio communication could not be warned that a cyclone was imminent. The *Yongala* probably foundered in the early hours of 24 March. When she became overdue at Townsville, an extensive search was launched. Apart from the body of the racehorse and some cargo, nothing was found.

An Australian minesweeper found her in 1943; she was identified as a shipwreck in 1947, but not positively identified as the *Yongala* until her safe was recovered in 1958. In 1983 the *Yongala* was established as a protected zone under Australia's Historic Shipwrecks Act. Special permits are required to dive the wreck and nothing can be disturbed within a 500m (1640ft) radius.

Today she is one of Australia's best dive sites, lying at 45 degrees on her starboard side in 27m (89ft) of water with her port side at 12m (40ft), the bow marking the deepest point. Although the rigging has broken away, the hull is mostly intact. The only shelter in a large expanse of sea, the *Yongala* has become a haven for an amazing variety of marine life including an abundance of enormous fish.

Best treated as several dives, it is wise to descend the mooring line hand-over-hand until one reaches the lee of the wreck, and once there, divers should be careful that they are not swept off into open water. There are some human remains, crockery, cutlery, lamps, toilets and baths. The hull is covered with soft and stony corals, sponges, sea fans, sea whips and oysters, but it is the fish that grab one's attention.

Shoals of batfish, jacks, Rainbow Runners, snappers, Barracuda, soldierfish and unusual in shoals, Cobia appear to come out to greet divers. Stingrays jostle for position as they search out food, Eagle Rays, Permits, Napoleon Wrasse, Cat Sharks, Coral Groupers, moray eels, sea snakes and Wobbegongs are common, while Bull Sharks, Guitar Sharks and various reef sharks may be seen receding into the distance. Turtles check divers out and several enormous Queensland subspecies of Giant Groupers wait to be cleaned on the sand.

The phenomenal fish population and luxuriant marine growth are fed by strong currents that can be a challenge, the visibility can drop from 30m (100ft) to 5m (16ft) in a few minutes and surface conditions can often be so rough that diving is not possible.

OPPOSITE *In good conditions, the steamship* Yongala, *which lies off the coast of Queensland, is one of the best wreck dives in the world.*
BELOW *Divers often use a dive light to bring out the colours of the marine life on wrecks.*
BELOW *A diver comes face to face with a large stingray on the wreck of the* Yongala.

President Coolidge, Vanuatu

The *President Coolidge* is the largest easily accessible shipwreck in the world. Measuring 199m (654ft) long, 25m (81ft) wide and displacing 32,447 tonnes, she was built in 1931 by Newport News Shipbuilding & Dry Dock Company of Newport News, Virginia, USA. Launched on 21 February 1931, she was delivered to American President Lines on 1 October 1931 and operated as a luxury liner carrying almost 3500 passengers, mostly on trans-Pacific routes.

In 1942 the ship was adapted to carry large numbers of troops. She was heading for Luganville, in present-day Vanuatu, when on the morning of 26 October, just a short distance from her destination, she struck two American mines in the east entrance of the Segond Channel at Espiritu Santo. The captain tried to save the vessel by driving onto the reef at full speed but she continued to take on water, slipped off and sank. Of the 5440 troops and crew on board, only two died.

The ship lies on her port side at depths from 15–70m (50–230ft) with the bow at the shallowest point and the stern the deepest. Being so large and in parts so deep, divers require several dives to cover it in detail, combining as it does, the furnishings of an advanced luxury liner for its time and the equipment of war. Divers new to the wreck can get a feeling of her immense proportions by starting at the promenade deck where light streaming through openings gives atmosphere.

A favourite with many divers is 'The Lady', a ceramic figure of a woman with a unicorn which used to stand above a marble fireplace, down one level at 45m (150ft), at the far end of the First Class Smoking Room. It was not discovered until 1981, and the wreck has been a marine sanctuary since 1969, so it was protected.

Unfortunately, a large part of it broke away and fell off during a recent earth tremor. Local dive operators gathered the broken pieces together, rebuilt the ceramic and repositioned it in a more accessible place for visiting divers – they bolted it to the ceiling of the First Class Dining Saloon at 39m (128ft).

On the bottom, at around 42m (138ft), there are 20mm (0.8in) cannons and the massive anchor lies in the sand. From the swimming pool, divers can swim though the main lounge area and exit through the bridge. The holds contain artillery, munitions, trucks, jeeps, medical supplies, urns, pots, pans and plates, while the deck is littered with gas masks, rifles and submachine guns. The engine room is entered through a large hole cut for salvage work and everything inside is carpeted with algae. The wreck shelters shoaling barracuda and jacks, Moray Eels, angelfish, butterflyfish, Coral Groupers and parrotfish, and for macro photographers there are nudibranchs, cleaner shrimps and arrow crabs.

For those competent enough to dive the stern, one normally descends down a shot- or mooring-line to the two propeller shafts (the propellers were salvaged in the 1970s), and the single rudder. The rear 130mm (5in) gun is still pointing over the stern.

Most dives on the *President Coolidge* are treated as decompression dives, with spare scuba cylinders of air or Nitrox hung at 5 and 9m (16 and 30ft) or deeper, on a line that stretches down to the bow at 20m (65ft). Local divemasters have fed the fish in the past while decompressing so they now approach divers expectantly. Although you do not need to be really experienced to dive the easier sections of the *President Coolidge,* deep penetration lengthwise and dives to the stern are only for very experienced and competent divers with a thorough understanding of decompression. Dives deeper than 50m (165ft) are beyond the depth recommended for diving on air by most training agencies.

OPPOSITE TOP *An old lamp globe on* the President Coolidge, Vanuatu, *is illuminated by a diver's torch.*
OPPOSITE BOTTOM *A diver swims past portholes on the* President Coolidge.
ABOVE *'The Lady', one of the best-known artefacts on the* President Coolidge.

ABOVE *The stern section of the* Proteus, *showing the propeller and rudder, looms out of the cold Atlantic off Cape Hatteras.* BELOW Duane *prior to sinking and shortly after being sunk. Divers were in the water at the time of the scuttling and surveyed the wreck once she had settled onto the seabed.*

Proteus, Duane and *Bibb,* East Coast, USA

The US East Coast is one of the world's most active wreck diving areas. From Massachusetts to Florida there is a scattered collection of ships from many eras, including colonial Spanish galleons, warships from the American Civil War, merchant ships and submarines from World War II and commercial vessels from throughout American history. Because of the offshore locations of most of the popular wrecks, the depths and the rather rugged diving conditions, much, although not all, East Coast wreck diving is reserved for more experienced divers. In fact, the American technical diving community developed chiefly among the serious East Coast wreck divers, together with the cave diving enthusiasts of Florida.

PROTEUS

Off the coast of North Carolina is an area known as 'the Graveyard of the Atlantic', so named because of the hundreds of ships that have sunk there over the centuries. More than 120 wrecks are frequented by dive charter boats. Divers find the diving exciting, with somewhat gentler conditions than found further to the north. Located in the warm Gulf Stream that flows up the coasts of Florida and the Bahamas, in the late summer months water temperatures are comfortable and the marine life includes many tropical species, such as angelfish, butterflyfish and groupers.

One of the most impressive wrecks in the area is the 125m (406ft) steamer, the *Proteus.* Sunk in a collision in 1918, she lies in 39m (125ft) of water, some 40km (25 miles) south of Hatteras Inlet. The superstructure amidships rises nearly 15m (50ft) off the bottom, and steel spars and huge boilers lie scattered on the sand. Perhaps the most exciting aspect of the *Proteus,* however, is its unusual marine life – in the autumn (fall) months (October–November) the wreck is the gathering place for large shoals of Sand Tiger (Raggedtooth) Sharks that mill about, willing to be approached quite closely by divers. Despite their fearsome, snaggle-toothed appearance, the sharks are docile and nonthreatening.

DUANE AND BIBB

In the clear, warm waters off the Florida Keys, the twin wrecks of the *Duane* and the *Bibb* provide thrills for both experienced, deep-water wreck divers and sport divers without wreck experience. The two ships are 100m-long (327ft) US Coastguard cutters that were sunk in 1987 to create artificial reefs. Both wrecks were environmentally cleaned and prepared for divers before being submerged, and they provide excellent dives in generally ideal conditions.

The *Duane* sits upright on the bottom at 27m (90ft), but her crow's nest reaches within 15m (50ft) of the surface. The *Bibb,* which lies in 40m (130ft) of water just .8km (half a mile) to the north, is a deeper wreck and is very popular with technical divers.

Currents on the wrecks can be strong at times, and divers tend to descend to the wrecks by means of a shotline linking the wrecks to a surface buoy. Once at the wrecks, divers should start out by swimming against the current, and then when the dive ends, they can use it to drift back to the shotline to start their ascent.

Underwater visibility often exceeds 30m (100ft), giving spectacular views of the huge vessels, which have been colonized by a wide variety of marine life, including shoals of barracuda, grouper and, on occasion, Eagle Rays.

LEFT *A dragging anchor caused the Bibb to settle on her starboard side, so although she is an identical vessel to Duane, the dive profile is different.*
BELOW *The Gulf Stream current almost always flows over the Duane, creating conditions of superb visibility. Shoals of grunts have made their home on both wrecks, and eagle rays may also be seen at times.*

ABOVE *Lengthy decompression stops are part of deep diving.*
These divers have a load of crockery salvaged from the wreck
of the Andrea Doria, *off Nantucket Island, USA.*
BELOW *The* Andrea Doria *carried enough crockery for 400*
tables. This Second Class china was found inside a stairwell.
BELOW RIGHT *A diver scrapes clean the letter 'E' on the stern of*
the Andrea Doria.

DEEP WRECKS

The wrecks featured on these pages are beyond the limits of normal recreational diving, as they require advanced skills and specialized equipment. However, as technical barriers continue to be broken, it is likely that more divers will achieve the necessary skills to explore these and other deep wrecks.

Andrea Doria, Nantucket Island, USA

The queen of American wreck diving, the cruise ship *Andrea Doria* lies 73km (45 miles) south of Nantucket Island, Massachusetts. The 212m-long (697ft) flagship of the Italian Line sank on 25 July 1956 after the Swedish-American Line's MV *Stockholm* rammed into her in dense fog, killing 46 of the *Andrea Doria's* passengers and five of the *Stockholm's* crew. Fortunately the *Andrea Doria* took 11 hours to sink and the tragedy took place near enough to New York for rescue operations. The *Stockholm* limped into port.

The following day, Peter Gimbel and Joseph Fox located the buoy left by the coastguard and became the first to dive the wreck. Gimbel's black-and-white photographs were sold to *Life* magazine, which then hired him to take colour pictures, so two-weeks later, a full-scale *Life* magazine expedition dived the wreck. Gimbel returned five times during the next 25 years, sharing his fascination for the ship with the public through pictures and films. In 1981 he managed to raise one of the ship's safes and stored it in the New York Aquarium's shark tank until it could be opened 'live' on national television. It contained US silver certificates and Italian banknotes.

Today, the wreck lies on her starboard side in 73m (240ft) of water with unpredictable currents. For many years, divers who explored the wreck had to endure nitrogen narcosis, nowadays they reduce this by using Trimix or Heliox, but sharks and decompression stops are still a major part of the dive.

The *Andrea Doria* is neither the deepest wreck, nor the largest, but it has mystique and has become known as the American divers' premier challenge – the 'Mount Everest' of wreck diving. US wreck diving specialist, Gary Gentile, has logged more than 100 dives on the ship.

The *Britannic*, Athens, Greece

The HMHS *Britannic*, sister ship to the *Olympic* and *Titanic*, was being used as a World War I hospital ship when she sank after a mysterious explosion in the busy Kéa shipping lane south of Athens on 21 November 1916. Thirty of the 1134 people on board died, mostly because their lifeboats were sucked under when the captain restarted the propellers, unaware that the crew had already deployed the boats.

Captain Jacques-Yves Cousteau located the wreck in December 1975, but it was September 1976 before he could dive her, using commercial diving systems and a diving bell.

In July 1995, commercial diver Kostas Thoctarides used open-circuit technical diving on a single, solo dive and in August/September 1995, the discoverer of the *Titanic*, Robert Ballard, ran an expedition to the *Britannic* that was subsidized by a television film contract and by the US Navy, with the loan of a Survey Vessel and a submarine – but no divers were used. Filming from the submarine was limited due to the dangers presented by fishing nets caught on the wreck.

In October and November 1997, Kevin Gurr led a team of recreational Trimix divers to the wreck. With a depth of 120m (394ft) giving decompression times of 3–4 hours among large ships, a Rigid Inflatable Boat (RIB) was used as a floating decompression platform. On ascent the divers made their fist stop at 70m (230ft) and their second at 60m (197ft). They stopped and switched to air at 51m (167ft), to Nitrox 40 at 30m (98ft) and to Nitrox 80 at 9m (30ft). The last stops were made at 9m (30ft), 6m (20ft) and 4.5m (15ft).

The *Lusitania*, Kinsale, Ireland

The largest and fastest vessel of her time, the Cunard Line's RMS *Lusitania* was torpedoed by the German submarine U-20 on 7 May 1915, 19km (12 miles) south of Ireland's 'Old Head of Kinsale'. The death toll was over 1200, including 291 women, 94 children and a number of American VIPs.

First dived in 1935 by Jim Jarrett using a forerunner of the armoured one-atmosphere diving suit, the Royal Navy dived her in 1954 and her owner, John Light, dived her in the late 1960s and early 1970s.

The anchors and three of her four propellers were salvaged in 1982 by divers using Heliox. Robert Ballard surveyed her with submersibles and Remotely Operated Vehicles in 1993, but it was 1994 before recreational divers first visited the *Lusitania* under the leadership of Polly Tapson. The mostly British team invited four Americans, including wreck diving expert Gary Gentile, to join them. With the wreck lying on her starboard side at 93m (305ft), each diver used twin 15-litre (120 cu ft) back-mounted cylinders containing Trimix plus two side-mounted 10-litre (80 cu ft) cylinders containing travel/decompression Nitrox. For decompression, Nitrox 32, Nitrox 50 and pure oxygen were used. One oxygen cylinder per diver, each with its own regulator, was hung at 6m (20ft) for final decompression.

In September 1998, John Chatterton and Innes McCartney became the first divers to have dived the *Andrea Doria*, *Lusitania* and *Britannic*. Chatterton also became the first diver to use a rebreather on the *Britannic*, while Christina Campbell became the deepest female wreck diver ever.

ABOVE *The* Britannic *prior to launching. When the* Titanic *sank,* Britannic *was under construction. Modifications were made to her watertight bulkheads and a double-skin was added, yet she took just 57 minutes to sink, three times faster than the* Titanic.

BELOW *A chain protrudes from the remains of a window on the* Lusitania.

EXTENDED RANGE (TECHNICAL) DIVING

Extended range, or technical, diving employs a range of gas mixtures other than normal air to reduce the problems associated with nitrogen and oxygen under pressure. Recreational divers require detailed training before these gas mixtures can be used.

NITROX

Nitrox is oxygen-enriched air. By increasing the percentage of oxygen and thus decreasing the percentage of nitrogen, divers will absorb less nitrogen during a dive and have less to eliminate during the ascent. Diving on Nitrox can be treated several ways: by calculating dive plans from Nitrox tables, divers will have longer no-decompression stop times at their maximum depth; if calculating dive plans from air tables, they will have an extra safety factor. If divers go into decompression, it will be shorter if calculated from Nitrox tables, or have a greater safety factor if calculated from air tables.

Alternatively, divers who have been deep while breathing air or other gas mixtures can shorten decompression times at shallow depths by changing to a mixture containing 50–80 percent oxygen to give faster elimination of excess helium or nitrogen.

However, due to oxygen toxicity, the depths that divers can descend to depend on the percentage of oxygen in the Nitrox mix used. The higher the percentage of oxygen, the shallower they will be able to dive to. Divers should not descend to depths where the partial pressure of oxygen exceeds 1.4ata. Similarly, oxygen breathed at higher partial pressures over long periods affects the central nervous system and divers must be careful not to exceed the recommended oxygen tolerance units (OTUs), particularly on repetitive dives.

High concentrations of oxygen cause combustion on contact with oils and greases. Scuba cylinders and their valves have contact with pure oxygen during filling, so they must be scrupulously clean. Regulators should be suitable for Nitrox mixtures of less than 40 percent oxygen, but for higher concentrations, their O-rings must be replaced with ones that do not require grease.

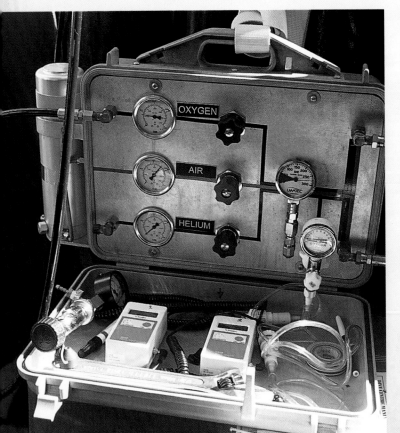

HELIOX AND TRIMIX

For deeper diving, as well as reducing the nitrogen content, one must also lower the oxygen content to reduce oxygen toxicity. This is done by replacing some of the Nitrogen with helium (Trimix) or all of the nitrogen with helium (Heliox). Helium has advantages over the problems caused by nitrogen narcosis, but not over decompression times. Being a lighter element than nitrogen, more of it is absorbed by the body and then has to be eliminated. It also conducts heat away from the body more quickly during respiration.

As divers go deeper, they must reduce the oxygen content still further. There is almost an optimum mix for each depth. Divers use a travel-mix suitable for breathing from the surface down to a reasonable depth, and then switch over to a bottom-mix with even lower oxygen content. However, bottom-mixes have too low an oxygen content to be breathed safely at shallower depths. During ascent, there will be a depth at which divers must switch back to the travel-mix. Shallow decompression stops will be shorter if they switch to mixes high in oxygen close to the surface.

Such dives rely on divers having several cylinders of different gas mixtures and being able to identify the correct regulator attached to the correct cylinder for each phase of the dive. This has led to the development of modern rebreathers, in which the gas mixture can be modified as one varies depth.

The future of diving would appear to be rebreathers. Divers breathe a mixture containing oxygen, and a 'scrubber' of Soda Lime chemically absorbs the carbon dioxide from the exhaled gases. More oxygen is then added and divers rebreathe the mix. Closed-circuit systems only dump gas that expands on ascent, while semi-closed circuit systems only dump a small portion of each breath, so divers get long diving times from a small amount of breathing gas.

Rebreathers can be based on Nitrox or, for deeper diving, Trimix or Heliox. They require considerable maintenance and users must keep a constant eye on their gauges to make sure everything is working correctly.

OPPOSITE TOP *A technical diver wearing a back-mounted rebreather and carrying extra waist-mounted scuba cylinders.*

OPPOSITE BOTTOM *Diving with mixed gases (such as Heliox or Trimix) requires specialized equipment and training.*

ABOVE *Divers decompressing on a line just below the surface; the line gives them an accurate depth.*

LEFT *A diver wearing modern rebreather equipment and a full-face mask.*

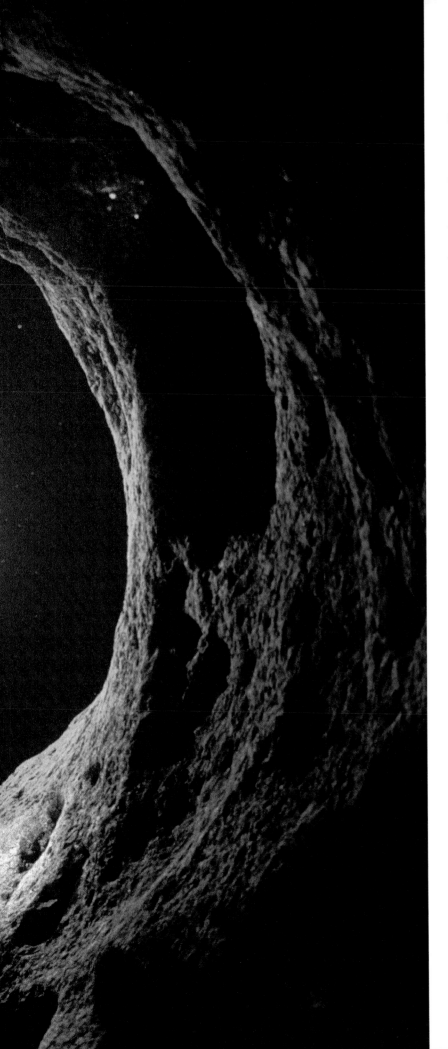

CLOSED OVERHEAD ENVIRONMENTS

WHEN DIVING IN ENCLOSED OVERHEAD ENVIRONMENTS, divers cannot easily reach the surface in the event of equipment failure. Cavern diving or easy wreck penetration, where divers are always within sight of daylight, are not difficult. However, deeper wreck penetration or true cave diving, beyond any source of daylight, requires the laying of a safety guideline so that the divers can find their way back to the entrance in zero visibility, as well as separate backup sources of light and air supply. Most important is the rule of thirds: divers turn around when one-third of their breathing gas is used up, leaving one-third to find their way out, and one-third for emergencies.

In cavern diving, divers enter caves but remain within sight of natural daylight and an exit. Daylight streaming through cavern openings creates stunning rays of light through the water and there are beautiful rock formations, fossils, and stalactites and stalagmites coloured by mineral deposits to view. A halocline forms where a layer of fresh water meets a layer of salt water, scattering the light and blurring the visibility as divers pass through it.

As with penetrating wrecks, cavern divers should learn how to streamline their equipment to avoid getting it tangled up with anything such as guidelines, and how to handle a free-flowing regulator, good buoyancy control and gentle finning from the ankles to avoid stirring up too much silt. The rule of thirds for air supply is not necessary, but it is worth learning how to carefully lay a safety guideline that is tight, has reliable tie-off points and does not have to be crossed over so that it can be easily followed in zero visibility by letting it run through the fingers.

When diving under ice, the main problems are equipment failure and, in many instances, losing sight of the entrance hole or the entrance hole closing up during the dive, so ice divers should have two completely separate sources of air and be tethered to a line that runs through the entrance hole.

The line to which divers are attached should be strong enough for hauling them back to the surface hole in case of an emergency. Each line should be tied off to a stake or other immovable object such as a tree, and attended by someone whose sole job is to tender that line, feeling for an agreed series of rope signal pulls from the diver. The suggested signals are:

Surface crew's signal pulls	Diver's response
One – *Are you okay?*	One – *Yes, I am okay.*
Two – *Do you require more line?*	Two – *Yes.*
Three – *There is no more line.*	
Four or more – *Emergency*	Four – *Emergency; Pull me up.*

Erratic pulls, unreadable pulls or no response all signal an emergency, so the diver should be pulled up. The surface crew will constantly have to remove ice to keep the hole from freezing over. In some areas the ice is continually closing up or cracking open, so the crew should also watch out for this. In Arctic areas, where Polar Bears are possible, the surface crew should also be armed. In the water, the divers should never lose sight of the hole through the ice; usually there is bright light that indicates the entrance hole, but in lakes or during plankton blooms there may not be. In this situation, lower a scuba cylinder fitted with a regulator and a flashing (strobe) light. At sea, the ice could be constantly moving and tides still operate.

CLOSED OVERHEAD ENVIRONMENTS

PREVIOUS PAGES *At the Moon Pool Cavern, Isla del Aire, Menorca, divers swim through a phreatic tube to reach a smaller cave.*

OPPOSITE *Exploratory cave divers carry large amounts of backup equipment, and must ensure that they have sufficient air to cope with any emergency.*

ABOVE *The Bahamas' famous Blue Holes formed when the roofs of water-filled caves collapsed, producing deep lakes on land or openings inside the fringing reefs.*

TOP RIGHT *Cave divers often have to pull themselves through narrow passages, so good buoyancy control and gentle finning will help prevent silt being stirred up.*

BOTTOM RIGHT *This diver has turned his world upside down - he is standing on the underside of the ice in McMurdo Sound, Antarctica.*

ABOVE *At Tom's Belfry, Menorca, divers can swim up a phreatic tube.*
OPPOSITE TOP *The Coral Galleries are a series of caverns hollowed out of the reef at three different levels.*
OPPOSITE BOTTOM *Illuminated by the diver's light, these stalactites and stalagmites create an ethereal underwater landscape.*

Cavern diving, Menorca

Menorca, one of Spain's Balearic Islands, has many fine cavern dive sites. Some are tunnels with dead ends but others are larger chambers, often with smaller shafts branching off. As some of these are easier versions of more difficult caverns and caves, they are used for cavern diving speciality courses.

Pont d'en Gil Cavern has only a few places where daylight cannot be distinguished. There are two entrances; one where divers swim through constrictions and the main entrance, some 20m (65ft) wide and 18m (60ft) high, where rocks that have fallen from the cave roof litter the floor. The system is 220m (720ft) long. A layer of fresh water covers the sea water throughout the cavern and, in calm conditions at the entrance, the interface between the two reflects daylight further into the cavern than normal.

Progressing further into the cavern, stalactites, stalagmites and columns appear both below and above water. If the halocline is disturbed, the light from divers' underwater lights is reflected in all directions. Divers can also leave the water and explore the beautiful dry part of the cavern.

Menorca's largest cavern, Cathedral Cavern at Cap d'en Font, is not quite so beautiful but the entrance archway is 183m (600ft) high and 12m (40ft) wide, and the whole cavern is illuminated with soft light.

At Tom's Belfry, divers can swim up a phreatic tube – a tube formed during a volcanic eruption, from which steam or mud is expelled as a result of the sudden heating of underground water when it comes into contact with hot magma or rock. The divers' vision becomes blurred as they pass through the halocline and then enter an air pocket.

The Coral Galleries at the Isla del Aire near S'Algar are on a reef hollowed out on three levels. There are many entrances through which daylight illuminates the walls and roof, which are carpeted with delicate corals, encrusting sponges and miniature anemones. There are eight large caverns and many smaller ones on the Isla del Aire alone. One of them, the Moon Pool Cavern, begins horizontally then turns upward through an often-photographed phreatic tube to a small cave.

With a varied and healthy fish and invertebrate life as well as the rock formations, the caverns of Menorca offer a fine diving experience.

ABOVE Mexico's Yucatán coastline is the home to a number of natural wells, called cenotes, formed when the roofs of lime-stone caverns collapsed due to erosion over the centuries. RIGHT The accessible Carwash Cenote contains tetra and other freshwater fish whose sharp teeth can be a problem for divers. OPPOSITE TOP AND BOTTOM The visibility in El Grande Cenote is remarkable, but the stalactites and stalagmites are fragile, so good buoyancy is essential.

Cenote diving, Yucatán Peninsula, Mexico

Suspended in the water filling the huge collapsed cavern of El Grande, one of Mexico's many cenotes (natural wells), divers become entranced by the sun's rays shining through gaps between the water lilies on the surface. Apart from a small halocline, the water is always crystal-clear and often in the distance you can make out snorkellers around the entrance. There is sufficient light to see the stalactites and stalagmites, although they look even better in the beam of a dive light, as this brings out their colours.

Freshwater cave diving is at the technical forefront of diving but it is often a logistical nightmare. Equipment regularly has to be carried across rugged moun-tains or dense forests and, having reached the cave entrance, it then needs to be transported through several passages and even lugged along on a series of under-water dives to reach the point where the actual exploration begins.

However, an effortless type of freshwater cavern diving does exist. The Yucatán Peninsula divides the Caribbean Sea from the Gulf of Mexico at the southeastern tip of Mexico. As with most rainfall, the water drains to the sea but, as there are no surface streams or rivers in this area, all fresh water flows through underground cave systems. Cenotes occur where the porous limestone roofs of caverns have collapsed, exposing the water to the surface.

Formed by fast-flowing water, these cave systems dried out during the last ice age when the sea level dropped 100m (330ft). Rain then percolated through the ground, forming beautiful flow stones, stalactites and stalagmites in the systems, which today make astonishing displays. As sea levels rose again, the complex filled with crystal-clear water.

All cenotes are on private land and some have changing huts or platforms at the water's edge. Many can be accessed by road and enjoyed by less-experienced divers, so long as they remain within sight of the sunlight and do not dive too deep. Guided cavern diving tours exist or you can take a cavern diving course. Despite the usually excellent visibility, it is possible for silt to get stirred up and for

equipment to malfunction. For this reason, divers should use a continuous safety guideline fixed from outside the cavern, limit their depth to 30m (100ft) and their linear distance from the entrance to 60m (200ft). As well as relying on daylight, they should have a powerful battery-powered light to enable them to enjoy the scenery and at least one backup light powered by alkaline, not nickel-cadmium batteries. Underwater lights powered by nickel-cadmium batteries give no warning that their charge is about to go out, which can happen very suddenly. Backup lights are best powered by alkaline batteries, which dim slowly as their charge runs down.

The most easily accessible and popular cenote, called Carwash, is a huge, spectacular cavern, that is very safe if taken as a guided dive. The Temple of Doom is more adventurous, requiring a short walk through the jungle and descent by ladder into the water. A guideline allows exploration of the cavern at a depth that is never more than 30m (100ft) from the surface. There are at least four passages leading off from the main cavern but these require training in full cave-diving as divers will be out of the sight of daylight. Dos Ojos, two huge caverns connected by a passage only 7.5m (24ft) deep, has exceptionally clear water and the scenery is stunning. Sac Actun is only 14m (45ft) deep but it has thousands of beautiful formations and over 5000m (16,400ft) of explored passages. El Grande Cenote is beautiful and fragile so good buoyancy control is essential, but the clear water is great for photography.

Hardier cave divers, using full cave-diving techniques and underwater scooters in the passages connecting some of the cenotes, have explored and mapped what is believed to be one of the longest underground rivers in the world.

Gunter's Cathedral, Coron Island, Philippines

Just north–northeast of Calis Point on Coron Island in the Philippines, several under-cut limestone cliffs have caverns and keyholes. Having found the correct large underwater cavern, the divemaster will swim over coral-encrusted fallen rocks, enter the cavern and head for the lowest point of the floor. At first one cannot understand the divemaster's actions; there is a very narrow cleft in the cavern floor at 7–8m (23–26ft) but it looks to be no more than a dark cleft with a dead end. The divemaster will squeeze into the cleft until he disappears. Surprised, the following divers switch on their lights and one by one follow tentatively. At the far end of the cleft they will find a narrow tunnel and swimming carefully along it, see that it contains numerous Spiny Lobsters and Cowrie shells. Suddenly they realize that they can no longer see daylight and it is too narrow to turn back; they must either continue or reverse out blind.

Continuing, they eventually notice a gleam of light ahead, and soon they emerge from the tunnel at the bottom of a large chamber some 20m (65ft) high and slightly narrower in width. There is a hole in the roof where a medium-sized tree was growing until it broke the roof away and fell through into the chamber. Shafts of sunlight shine through this hole, descending vertically through the water and falling on the dead tree trunk and walls of the cavern. The divers will usually be spellbound. Their movements and exhaust bubbles cause the water surface to ripple and this in turn causes the shafts of sunlight refracted in the water to flicker about – the effect of sunlight in the cavern is surreal. The chamber itself is roughly one-third full of water, so divers can rise to the surface and chat to each other about it in air. This is Gunter's Cathedral, a unique and beautiful site originally discovered by local diving supremo Gunter Bernert.

Divers who wish to try this dive should not suffer from claustrophobia, must have steady nerves when in confined spaces and preferably be accompanied by an experienced local divemaster. The entrance tunnel is narrow enough to cause some divers to touch the walls and those with poor buoyancy control will stir up the sediment. On a flood tide, the sediment fills the tunnel, making it very difficult for divers to find their way out again. Although this site is a cavern in the diving sense of the word because it has daylight, getting to it involves an element of cave diving where divers are temporarily out of sight of the daylight. It is worth using a safety guideline from the open sea. Outside, there is interesting coral, anemones, clownfish and true Giant Clams for those wary of following down the tunnel.

There is no indication from the surface or from underwater that the cavern is there. Newcomers rely on a local divemaster or boatman being able to recognize the rock structure of the cliffs above, although GPS receivers are increasingly utilized.

BELOW *Cliffs above Gunter's Cathedral, Coron, Philippines.*
OPPOSITE *Light streams into Gunter's Cathedral - a water-filled cavern with a hole in the roof above water and the entrance below water.*

Blue Holes, Bahamas

Despite the lack of surface rivers today in the Bahamas, most of the islands have extensive cave systems that often stretch for several kilometres and reach underwater depths beyond 100m (330ft). During the ice ages, when water levels were much lower, caves were formed by acidic rainwater dissolving the surface limestone. When the water level of the oceans rose, these caves filled with water. Where the caves had become too large to support their roofs, they collapsed to produce lakes on land or deep, blue-black openings inside the fringing reef – today's Blue Holes of the Bahamas.

Scattered throughout the islands, the blue holes form deep, circular cenotes (similar to those in Yucatán) on land or irregular entrances off the coast. Serious exploration of these caves began on Andros in the late 1950s with Canadian George Benjamin and his team, who in 1967 found Benjamin's Blue Hole, a large system on the South Bight of Andros. Both Benjamin and Jacques-Yves Cousteau made documentary films within the cave system, and the existence of the Bahamas Blue Holes was broadcast to the world.

On Grand Bahama, American cave divers found the Lucayan Caverns, which have over 8km (5 miles) of passages, and biologist Jill Yager discovered a new order of marine life, Remipedia, a group of crustaceans thought to have become extinct over 150 million years ago. Many new species have been discovered in these blue holes and the skeletons of several Lucayan Indians and a Lucayan canoe – possibly 1000 years old – were found in some of the holes on South Andros.

Oceanic blue holes can have strong tidal currents, causing strong vortexes as they blow and suck, so visibility is usually best on an outflowing tide. In inland blue holes, although water levels rise and fall with the tides, no current occurs. Uniquely a layer of fresh water lies on top of ocean salt water. Debris from surrounding vegetation falls into the water and decays, producing tannic acid and hydrogen sulphide, which reduces visibility at the surface. Divers descend through this layer and, in some instances, several thermoclines and chemoclines, and the halocline into clear salt water.

Mosquitofish, a species found only in the Bahamas, shoal near the surface feeding on insect larvae and zooplankton. Males transfer sperm to the females' bodies using a modified fin called a gonopodium and the females, instead of laying eggs, give birth to live, free-swimming young. Some inland blue holes have needlefish, Grey Snappers and blue crabs, originally marine species but now adapted to living in brackish water. The Blue Hole Cave Fish is a member of a family normally found deep in the ocean but here it has adapted to shallower marine cave systems.

Blue holes where the diving is suitable only for experienced divers have permanent safety guidelines with direction markers. The 'mung', the bacterial debris on the cave floor, is easily stirred up, so divers should clip their own lines onto the fixed line before moving away from it, wear fully redundant cave diving equipment (essential items that are duplicated as a precaution against failure) and be properly trained in its use.

Along passageways, divers' exhaust bubbles will dislodge particles from the ceiling and in some instances, access by non-scientific divers is restricted in order to protect the caves, but at Guardian Blue Hole the surface visibility ranges from 1.5–9m (5–30ft) and becomes crystal-clear around 27m (90ft). The passageway passes stalactites before leading into an enormous cavern. At Stargate Blue Hole, divers descend through the sulphur layer to 25m (80ft), where the safety guideline branches to run north and south. That branching to the north passes large stalactites and flow stone formations. When diving the blue holes, as well as appreciating their beauty, divers are witnessing nature in the process of evolution.

ABOVE *In this aerial view, an inshore Blue Hole stands out against the surrounding reef.*
BELOW *Rob Palmer negotiating a rock fall deep in the Lucayan Caverns on Grand Bahama.*

ABOVE A sign at the entrance to Sipadan's Turtle Cavern warns divers not to venture further without a trained guide.
BELOW The skeleton of a turtle picked clean by the tiny shrimps, crabs and worms found in Turtle Cavern.

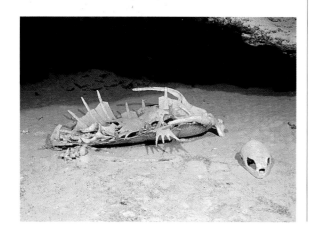

Turtle Cavern, Sipadan, Borneo

I have seen other places like Sipadan, 45 years ago. Now we have found again an untouched piece of art. The words of Jacques-Yves Cousteau, after Ron Holland of Borneo Divers had shown him the delights of diving Sipadan in Malaysian Borneo, guaranteed its popularity. Divers who decide to brave the linked underwater caverns of Sipadan will first swim over the drop-off just east of the main jetty and descend to a large cavern at 18m (60ft). Here, the divemaster will indicate that they do a final check on their equipment and turn on their lights, then he motions them to follow him towards the back of the cavern.

At first the cavern drops to 21m (70ft) and it appears as though the divers are heading for a blank wall but slowly they realize there is a passage rising from the rear of the cavern. Following the resort dive master up this tunnel, they soon understand why he is obligatory on this dive. No longer able to discern daylight, they cannot see their way out and without a safety guideline it is easy to become disoriented and lost. Divers not accompanied by a resort divemaster have got lost and died here.

Moving carefully to avoid disturbing the silt, the divers swim past the skeleton of a marlin, turn into another passage and then enter a larger chamber. They have prepared themselves for the turtle carapaces and skeletons that litter the floor – but the sight of the body of a turtle buoyed up at the roof by the gases of decomposition gives them a jolt. This is Sipadan's famous Turtle Cavern.

Romanticized as the place where turtles go to die, the reality is very different; the drop-off contains many caves, which turtles and Bumphead Parrotfish use to rest in. Some turtles venture so far into the limestone labyrinth that they can no longer see the light of the entrances. Unable to find their way out again, they get lost and, incapable of reaching the surface to breathe, they drown. The decomposing bodies then become the food that supports some unique shrimps, tiny transparent crabs and worms that have evolved to be able to live without daylight.

The various interconnecting passages reach 70m (230ft) inland at their farthest point from the main entrance and rise to within 4m (13ft) of the surface. Stalactites show that the caves were formed as a result of weathering during the last ice age when the sea level was some 100m (330ft) lower than at present.

For those new to cave diving, the fear of running out of air before they can find their way out produces an adrenaline rush. This instigates heavy breathing which leads to excessive use of the air in their scuba cylinders. Divers who cannot force themselves to calm down should abort the dive at the first passage that heads upwards. There are great photo opportunities in the passages that are further in, but as soon as one of the group indicates that a pressure gauge is reading below half-pressure, the divemaster will usher them out of the cavern and back to open water.

Some Sipadan resorts require that divers have passed a cave diving course before they allow them into Turtle Cavern, even with a divemaster; however, it is not necessary on such a short dive so long as a resort divemaster accompanies the divers all the way and limits how far they penetrate.

Wookey Hole, England

In Britain, the sumps (cave passages completely filled with water) that connect passages filled with air are often very constricted. It can also require expedition-type planning and portage of equipment over difficult underground terrain and through several sumps just to reach the point where the exploratory dive is to begin. The conditions in Wookey Hole, part of which is a tourist attraction in the Mendip Hills, Somerset, in the south west of England, are typical of this.

Often, when diving these sumps, on returning from the farthest point the underwater visibility is near-zero, and without enough room to share air the buddy system is not practicable. In fact, having two divers in the same narrow passage in near-zero visibility would cause extra problems. Divers have to be self-reliant with multiple redundancy, (backup of those items whose failure could cause death). Several lights are usually mounted on a protective helmet to keep the diver's hands free, but where there is back-scatter, a hand-light is preferable. Scuba cylinders are mounted on either side of the body for streamlining in low passages, for access if they become entangled in a guideline, access to the valves and easy removal for passing individually through constrictions. At least two completely independent sets of breathing equipment are carried, with both cylinders having entirely separate regulators. First stages are environmentally sealed against mud and grit; DIN screw-fittings are less likely to be damaged or dislodged than yoke-clamps (A-clamps) in narrow passages. Second stages are carried on cords around the neck for instant location if it is necessary to change from one to another.

ABOVE *At this resurgence entrance at Wookey Hole, the river briefly comes into the open before continuing underground.* BELOW *Cave divers often have to contend with poor visibility and narrow passages, as encountered by this diver in Wookey Hole, England.*

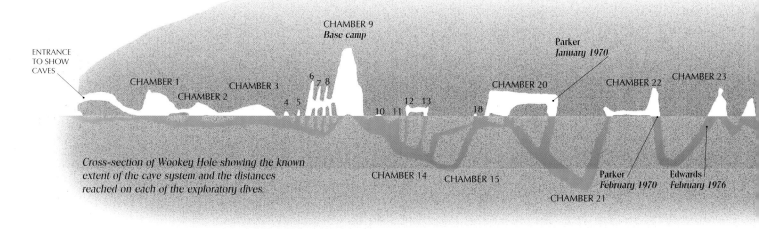

CHAMBER 9
Base camp

ENTRANCE
TO SHOW
CAVES

CHAMBER 1

CHAMBER 2

CHAMBER 3

CHAMBER 20

Parker
January 1970

CHAMBER 22

CHAMBER 23

6 7 8

4 5

10 11

12 13

18

CHAMBER 14

CHAMBER 15

CHAMBER 21

Parker
February 1970

Edwards
February 1976

*Cross-section of Wookey Hole showing the known
extent of the cave system and the distances
reached on each of the exploratory dives.*

TOP *Carefully-laid lines are essential so
that cave divers can find their way back
to the entrance in poor visibility.*
ABOVE *Cave divers must carry a great
deal of additional equipment, as safety
is paramount.*

CAVE DIVING – A MIRACULOUS SURVIVAL

The water was icy cold, the tunnel was black, but now for the first time I could see. I had emerged from a dense cloud of tannic water to visibility of 15 metres. This was my sixth cave dive and I was exploring in one of the longest caves in the country. I had been underwater for approaching eight minutes, and despite the tension, I was feeling pleased with my progress.

It was August 1971 and I was equipped with a single cylinder and a single light, a perfectly acceptable approach by the standards of the day. Cave diving was known to be a very risky business, but to a 20-year-old, a challenge such as this seemed of little consequence. The potential rewards far outweighed the dangers. As I swam, a thin orange line slowly dispensed from my home-made reel. A regular surge of bubbles rose past my mask. I could see exactly where I was going – along a water-carved corridor approximately four metres in diameter.

Then came the unexpected. I breathed out, but could not breathe in! The regulator, with its 'lifetime guarantee', had jammed shut! My brain was numbed; I grappled momentarily with the mouthpiece before elemental panic took over. All I knew was that there was no burst of life-giving air – either I got out fast or I was dead.

Minute silvery bubbles began to escape from the rubber valve in the face-plate of the mask, but these made no noise, the deathly silence of the ensuing minutes will never be forgotten. The line led me into a muddy 'squeeze' barely 30 centimetres high; here I succumbed to the craving and pulled my mouthpiece out. I began to breathe water. Everything I had learned was forgotten in the utter desperation of the situation. I resigned myself to fate. In another minute or so the struggle was over, I lay there peacefully.

Miraculously I survived the ordeal that day, as I had two stand-by divers at base – but six or eight nondiving assistants waiting on the shore were confirmed in their decision to never dive in a cave, and neither my rescuer, nor the other stand-by diver, ever dived again!

Martyn Farr, author of The Darkness Beckons – The History and Development of Cave Diving, *is one of Britain and the world's most renowned cave divers. A full Cave, Cavern and Nitrox instructor, he has been at the cutting edge of cave exploration for over 25 years. Among his career achievements are many depth and distance records in cave diving. Farr has found more unexplored caves than anyone else in the UK, and has participated in successful expeditions to the USA, Bahamas, Borneo, Iran, Mexico and Turkey. He has been involved with cave diving training in China and Japan.*

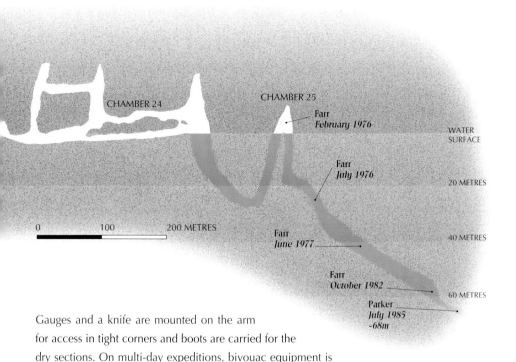

CHAMBER 24

CHAMBER 25

Farr
February 1976

WATER
SURFACE

Farr
July 1976

20 METRES

0   100   200 METRES

Farr
June 1977

40 METRES

Farr
October 1982

60 METRES

Parker
July 1985
-68m

ABOVE *Exploring Chamber 24 at Wookey Hole, 1982.*
BELOW *Divers kitting up beneath the tourist walkway in Chamber 9.*

Gauges and a knife are mounted on the arm for access in tight corners and boots are carried for the dry sections. On multi-day expeditions, bivouac equipment is also transported to a suitable overnight site.

Over the years, at Wookey Hole, as a result of gradual improvements in equipment, techniques, clothing, breathing and decompression gases, and the sheer dogged determination of a small number of fanatical cave divers, more and more of the sumps were passed. By 1971 cave divers had reached chamber 22 but had never explored further, until the cave management opened an artificial tunnel to chamber 9. This brought renewed efforts, particularly by British diver Martyn Farr. Using chamber 9 as a base, by February 1976 divers had passed chamber 25, having explored nearly 1km (half a mile) of dry cave and completed 610m (2000ft) of diving from chamber 9. Supported by other divers, who stockpiled air and oxygen at chamber 25, Farr made several further attempts in 1976, 1977 and 1982 – all pushing the limits. The saw-tooth profile of the dives to reach chamber 25 required repeating on the return, but beyond chamber 25 the water depths were seriously into those of nitrogen narcosis and decompression. Travel breathing mixes were devised for the approach sumps, a final mix for the final solo exploration and pure oxygen for decompression.

On each attempt Farr reached record depth levels for the UK, but the passage continued downward. On the 1982 attempt, the team took six hours to get from chamber 9 to chamber 25. Farr continued alone but was forced to turn back after nearly 300m (1000ft) because he had reached the predetermined depth of 60m (200ft), and the roof had closed to within 35cm (1ft) of the floor. After the required decompression stops, Farr surfaced to join the support team in chamber 25 and breathed pure oxygen there for a while, before they made their way back to the overnight camp in chamber 24 to allow excess nitrogen to fully out-gas from his body before returning to the surface. In 1985, Rob Parker, diving on Trimix, reached a definite end of the cave system at a depth of 68m (223ft), only 9m (30ft) past Farr's previous effort.

ABOVE A typical dive site in the Antarctic, with a hut covering the hole and a Spryte (tracked vehicle) standing by.
BELOW Preparing to dive through a new hole at Hut No. 9, Arrival Heights, McMurdo Sound, Antarctica
OPPOSITE TOP LEFT Divers returning to the dive hut under cloud-like ice cover at Arrival Heights, McMurdo Sound.
OPPOSITE TOP RIGHT A golden sunset lights up Erebus Ice Tongue, McMurdo Sound.
OPPOSITE BOTTOM A diver under a safety hole at Little Razorback Island, McMurdo Sound

DIVING UNDER ICE

Ice diving requires specialized equipment and thorough preparation. Even the best equipment is liable to failure, so divers should be prepared. The water temperature cannot drop below -1.8°C (28.8°F) or it would be frozen solid, so the real problems are caused by the air temperatures, which can be several 10s of degrees colder, especially with wind-chill. Nowadays all ice divers wear drysuits with several layers of undergarments, gloves and a hood that covers as much of the face as possible. The resulting bulk requires considerable weight to neutralize the diver's buoyancy. In extreme conditions metal weight-belt buckles have been known to fail. Full-face masks are a problem, since, if the regulator fails, the diver cannot easily access a backup regulator.

For redundancy, divers should each have two completely separate regulators, either on separate scuba cylinders or on a single cylinder with a 'V'-manifold. The scuba cylinders should be filled with air that is as dry as possible, and cylinders and regulators should be stored out of the wind in a dry place until the divers enter the water. The regulator first stages should be environmentally sealed against the ingress of water and not be breathed through until both first and second stages are submerged, to avoid condensation freezing the regulator.

Ice diving can take place in a lead (a crack in the ice), or a hole cut through the ice, although ice movement can cause a lead to close, trapping the divers beneath thick ice. Where a hole is cut, a triangular shape will enable two divers to get in and out of the water simultaneously by using the sides of the hole at separate corners for leverage. Ideally there should be shelter beside or over the hole where divers can kit up and keep out of the wind. In its simplest form this would be a windbreak, but where possible it should be a vehicle or tent. Small items of equipment are easily lost in snow, so these need to be placed on a groundsheet or in a vehicle. Hot drinks and food should be available before and after the dive.

Diving under ice is a surreal experience. The ice forms amazing shapes, while animals at high latitudes exhibit gigantism, growing extremely slowly but living to an old age, and becoming much larger in the process.

McMurdo Sound, Antarctica

At first sight, McMurdo Sound in Antarctica seems an unlikely place to go scuba diving. Hurricane-force winds scour the frozen surface of the sea, air temperatures routinely plunge below -40°C (-40°F), and the wind chill can reach -90°C (-130°F). It's a world that seems entirely devoid of life. There are no insects, no plants, no large terrestrial flora or fauna of any kind. Yet McMurdo Sound has some of the most spectacular diving in the world.

McMurdo Sound lies between 77 and 78° south latitude in the Ross Sea. For most of the summer diving season (September–February), it is covered by a 1.3–3m-thick (4–10ft) blanket of ice. Divers break through this ice using a diesel-powered auger (boring tool), high explosives, or ice saws and ice chippers (used to widen naturally occurring cracks). The auger makes a 1.3m-diameter (4ft) hole that divers quickly cover with a portable hut. The hut not only keeps the new hole from freezing, but it also provides divers with a warm place to suit up. This is important, since exposed flesh freezes quickly and dive equipment is often rendered inoperable at -90°C (-130°F). Later in the austral (southern) summer, temperatures may rise

to as high as 2°C (35.6°F) and properly-clad divers can successfully operate outside. Even so, the water in McMurdo Sound remains at a nearly constant -1.8°C (28.8°F).

Because of the total ice cover and extreme temperatures, diving in Antarctica requires a high level of skill. Divers must be proficient in the use of dry suits, and they must also be able to manipulate their equipment while wearing the thick mitts needed to keep their hands from freezing. Normal ice diving procedures mandate that divers are securely tethered to the surface by an unbreakable line. However, in McMurdo Sound most divers do not use tether lines from September to November, as underwater visibility during that time of the year can be 300m (990ft), and divers are easily able to see their dive holes. Since it is nearly impossible to become lost under the ice, the tether is an unnecessary hindrance. Nonetheless, it is important for divers to maintain constant visual contact with the dive hole. In case of regulator failure, dry suit flood, or other emergency, they must be able to locate and reach the hole quickly.

To assist divers in maintaining visual contact with the dive hole, a down line is deployed through the hole before the dive. This line has a weight at the end that keeps it taut in the water column, and it is marked with checkered flags and strobe lights to increase its visibility. The down line also serves as a stable visual reference for moderating ascent rates, and as a platform for doing safety stops.

After all the necessary preparations, divers slipping into the frigid water are amply rewarded. The sea ice, backlit by the sun, forms a glowing, blue cover over the ocean. Everything else is dim and shadowy, since only about one per cent of incident sunlight penetrates the ice. However, once the eyes adjust, there's plenty of light, and the tremendous visibility gives divers the sensation that they are flying over a darkened landscape of hills, valleys and sheer cliffs.

Around volcanic Ross Island, which forms the eastern boundary of McMurdo Sound, the loose, rocky bottom slopes steeply into the depths. Between September and December, there is almost no current, and there is never any surge. Sometimes, though, supercooled water will push out from under the Ross Ice Shelf to the south, causing the water temperature to drop by one degree. This seemingly negligible drop in temperature has a profound effect on the environment. Ice crystals form in the water, creating the illusion of a million, tiny, floating diamonds. Requiring something to nucleate around, ice also forms by attaching itself to rocks on the bottom. This 'anchor' ice develops into a brittle blanket that covers the sea floor down to 15m (50ft). Only motile (moving) animals like sea stars, urchins, sea spiders, and isopods are able to exist here, since the anchor ice essentially scours away any sessile (permanently attached) life forms. As divers descend past 15m (50ft), they encounter beds of anemones and soft corals and perhaps even a few fast-growing sponges.

Where the Antarctic sea floor truly becomes alive, though, is below 30m (100ft). Life there can be as diverse and dense as in some tropical communities. Sponges are the most prevalent inhabitants, with over 300 Antarctic species currently identified. They take on every imaginable shape and colour, including bright yellow fingers, spiny 'cactus' sponges, brilliant red lobes, pink horns, green globes, knobby white vases, and giant volcano-shaped sponges big enough for a diver to fit inside.

Hundreds of other species inhabit the Antarctic sea floor, like brightly coloured sea stars, giant sea spiders, frilly white nudibranchs, huge tunicates, featherduster worms, molluscs the size and colour of tennis balls, proboscis worms, soft corals, anemones, hydroids, polychaete worms and sea cucumbers.

Fish are neither as numerous nor as diverse as one finds in warmer waters, since it takes a unique physiology to exist in freezing water. Each fish species in McMurdo Sound has one or more forms of natural antifreeze in its blood and tissues. Most of these fish are brown and less than 30cm (12in) long. They also tend to move slowly and can often be easily caught by hand.

On the western side of McMurdo Sound, away from Ross Island and along the shores of the continent, the sea floor tends to be composed of either granite or soft sediment. There, divers often find different creatures than they would around Ross Island, such as crinoids, scallops, pencil urchins, and different species of sponge.

Weddell Seals are also conspicuous inhabitants of the under-ice environment. They have special adaptations that permit them to survive below fast ice (ice that is nearly solid from shore to shore), including forward-angled incisors they use to keep their breathing holes open. Able to hold their breath for 90 minutes and dive to 700m (2300ft), these seals spend most of their lives underwater. They cruise through the dim world below the ice like ghosts, sometimes seeming to come out of nowhere to investigate a team of divers. Fortunately, they are only curious.

Because much of the diving in McMurdo Sound is deep, divers generally schedule generous safety stops into their dive plans. Many will spend this time in the shallows investigating underwater ice caves or strange ice formations, or just inflating their dry suits and standing upside down on the ice.

With no dangerous animals to be concerned about, the only potential hazards in Antarctica are the intense cold and limited surface access, but these are easily overcome by careful training and preparation. When the rules are followed, ice diving in Antarctica is as safe as any other form of diving. Although there is currently no recreational ice diving around the frozen continent, with increasing tourist activities it is probably only a matter of time before an enterprising operator schedules a dive trip. When that happens, it is not to be missed.

Top *Fish on a polychaete sponge at 20m (65ft), Cape Armitage, Ross Island.*
Above *Brown vase sponge at 30m (100ft), Granite Harbour.*
Left *Weddell Seal under the ice at Turtle Rock, McMurdo Sound.*

DIRECTORY

Star Rating

The dives mentioned in this book have been allocated a star rating to signify the minimum standard of experience required for a diver to be comfortable, unless diving with an instructor.

★ An entry level diver such as:
BSAC Club Diver/Ocean Diver
NAUI Scuba Diver & Advanced Scuba Diver
PADI Open Water & Advanced Open Water Diver
SAA Open Water Diver
SSI Open Water & Advanced Open Water Diver

★★ An experienced diver such as:
BSAC Sports Diver
NAUI Scuba Rescue Diver
PADI Rescue Diver
SAA Club Diver
SSI Advanced Open Water Diver

★★★ A well-experienced diver such as:
BSAC Dive Leader
NAUI Master Scuba Diver
PADI Dive Master
SAA Dive Leader
SSI Master Diver

★★★★ An advanced diver with a higher qualification than listed above. These divers would usually be qualified in the use of Nitrox, but this is not essential, so long as they are not actually using this gas.

★★★★★ A technical diver, fully qualified in the use of Trimix or Heliox and who is capable of remaining calm in difficult or emergency situations.

Legend:
BSAC – British Sub-Aqua Club
NAUI – National Association of Underwater Instructors
PADI – Professional Association of Diving Instructors
SAA – Sub Aqua Association
SSI – Scuba Schools International

UK AND MEDITERRANEAN

UK west coast - Basking Sharks
Star Rating: ★
Location: West coast of the UK, from Cornwall to Scotland.
Climate: Temperate with four seasons. Variable though more settled in summer when temperatures range from 20–25°C (68–77°F). May–Jul has most sun, Jul–Aug is warmest.
Water temperature: 12–13°C (54–55°F) in summer.
Visibility: 3–10m (10–33ft) when plankton is abundant, otherwise 15–20m (50–65ft).

Depth: Surface to 5m (16ft).
Snorkelling: Good with Basking Sharks.
Best time to go: May–Aug are best, but Basking Sharks have been sighted as early as mid-March and late as mid-October.
Getting there: By boat from the mainland. Options to fly or take a ferry to Ireland or the Isle of Man.
Quality of Marine Life: Basking Sharks are the main attraction.
Dive practicalities: Suitable for all divers.

Mediterranean - Menorca caverns
Star Rating: ★★
Location: Mediterranean island off Spain.
Climate: Generally pleasant and sunny, temperatures vary between 20°C (68°F) in winter and 29°C (84°F) in summer.
Water temperature: 15–25°C (50–77°F).
Visibility: 3–30m (10–100ft), the lower figure occurs when divers stir up the silt.
Depth of Dives: Surface to 20m (65ft) for caverns.
Snorkelling: Some caverns can be snorkelled from the entrance, the experience will be enhanced if the snorkellers carry underwater lights.
Best time to go: Mar–Nov though best from May–Oct. High season for non-diving holiday makers is Jul–Aug.
Getting there: Fly to Mahon or take a ferry from Barcelona on the Spanish mainland.
Quality of Marine Life: Healthy and varied.
Dive Practicalities: Divers must have a Spanish Diving Permit. Local dive centres can issue these on presentation of proof of diving qualifications, two passport-sized photographs and a current diving medical certificate.

RED SEA AND INDIAN OCEAN

Red Sea (Israel, Egypt, Sudan) - sharks, dolphins, Manta Rays and wrecks
Star Rating: ★ Manta Rays, dolphins, *Thistlegorm*, ★★ sharks, ★ to ★★★ *Umbria*.
Location: Hurghada and Sharm El Sheikh are departure points for Egypt, Port Sudan for Sudan.
Climate: Warm and dry on land in winter but it can be windy and cold at sea, average 20°C (68°F). Hot and dry in summer, average 35°C (95°F). Northern Egypt is much colder than the countries further south where it can be hot and humid on land in summer with temperatures reaching 47°C (117°F). More comfortable though humid at sea.
Water temperature: Egypt: 19°C (66°F) in winter, 25–27°C (77–81°F) in summer. Sudan averages 27°C (81°F) in winter and 28°C (82°F) in summer. It can resemble a hot bath on the surface beside reefs on summer afternoons.
Visibility: Averages over 30m (100ft).
Depth: Variable depending on dive site. Up to 36m (118ft) on wrecks.
Snorkelling: Good.
Best time to go: All sites can be dived all year but the better sites are offshore and the boat journey

can be very rough in winter. The best conditions on offshore sites are from May–Sep. Avoid August for sites south of Egypt as heavy rains in Ethiopia cause south winds and haboobs (sandstorms).
Getting there: Israel: fly via Ovda. Egypt: direct charter flights or connecting flights via Cairo, to Sharm El Sheikh or Hurghada. Sudan: air connections are unreliable, particularly onward from Khartoum to Port Sudan. Direct flights sometimes operate from Cairo or Rome in winter. The best way is to charter a live-aboard boat from Egypt.
Quality of Marine Life: Extremely good in Egypt while Sudan has the greatest species diversity and density in the Red Sea. Wreck divers may prefer to concentrate on exploration and photography.
Dive Practicalities: The *Thistlegorm*, and most of the *Umbria*, are suitable for all levels of diver. Penetration requires advanced skills, and an underwater light and backup light are essential. No spare diving equipment or alkaline batteries are available in Port Sudan so divers must be self-sufficient (even toilet paper may not always be obtainable).

Maldives - Sharks
Star Rating: ★
Location: Island group to the south of India.
Climate: Tropical summer climate year round, dry season Jan–Mar, wet season May–Oct. Daily average temp: max 30°C (86°F), min 25°C (77°F).
Best Time to Go: Jan–May and Sep–Nov.
Water Temperature: 28–30°C (82–86°F).
Visibility: Visibility is variable, dependent upon the tide. At high tide, it may reach 24m (80ft), but at low tide, it may be reduced to only 9m (30ft).
Getting There: International flights to Malé from Europe and Asia. Island resorts are reached by boat from Malé.
Quality of Marine Life: Tremendous variety of species, including turtles and many large fish. Corals, both soft and hard varieties, are plentiful.
Depth of Dives: The shark dives are held in water from 12–18m (40–60ft).
Snorkelling: Excellent snorkelling is available, but the shark dives are scuba experiences.
Diving Practicalities: Suitable for almost any level of diver. Conditions are very calm.

South Africa - Great White Sharks and Raggedtooth Sharks
Star Rating: ★ Cage dives, ★★ Raggedtooth Sharks.
Location: Cage diving with Great White Sharks along the Western Cape coast from Cape Town eastward to Mossel Bay. Diving with Raggedtooth and other sharks off the KwaZulu-Natal coast from south of Durban to the Mozambique border.
Climate: Mediterranean climate with winter rainfall in the Western Cape; warmer sub-tropical climate in KwaZulu-Natal (KZN).
Water temperature: 13–19°C (55–66°F) in the Cape; 21–22°C (70–72°F) in KwaZulu-Natal.
Visibility: 8–10m (26–33ft) in False Bay (Cape Town); up to 25m (82ft) off Aliwal Shoal (KZN).

Depth of Dives: Just below the surface for cage dives; from 5–30m (16–100ft) on Aliwal Shoal, reaching 26–40m (85–130ft) at Protea Banks.

Snorkelling: No.

Best time to go: Apr–Oct for cage diving with Great Whites in the Cape; Jun–Nov for Ragged-tooth Sharks at Aliwal Shoal and Protea Banks.

Getting there: Fly to Cape Town or Durban.

Quality of Marine Life: Emphasis is on sharks, but great species diversity on KZN reefs.

Dive Practicalities: Aliwal Shoal and Protea Banks are for experienced divers only.

Western Australia - Ningaloo Reef, Rowley Shoals and Scott Reef

Star Rating: ★

Location: Isolated offshore reefs in the far north of Western Australia.

Climate: Tropical, through relatively dry. Land temperatures range from 16–30°C (60–85°F) in winter and spring (Apr–Nov). Summers very hot and dry. Cyclone season from Nov–Apr.

Water temperature: 22–30°C (72–86°F).

Visibility: Variable. From 18–30m (60–100ft) at Ningaloo Reef.

Depth: From surface to as deep as preferred.

Snorkelling: At Ningaloo Reef and Rowley Shoals.

Best time to go: All year round. Apr–Jun for Whale Sharks. Aug–Sep for whale watching tours.

Getting there: Light plane or drive from Perth (very long distances between outback towns).

Quality of Marine Life: Superb, with sea snakes, sharks, Manta Rays, Potato Cod and Dugong. Ningaloo Reef is unique for Whale Sharks.

Dive practicalities: Shore dives within lagoons, boat dives to outer reefs.

South Australia - Great White Sharks

Star Rating: ★

Location: Dangerous Reef and Neptune Islands.

Climate: Unpredictable, can change quickly from a calm, warm 24°C (75°F) day to strong winds and temperatures around 12°C (54°F).

Water temperature: 14–20°C (57–68°F).

Visibility: 5–12m (15–40ft).

Depth of Dives: Mainly just below the surface but cages may be lowered to 12–30m (40–100ft).

Snorkelling: Only within cages.

Best time to go: Summer, from Feb–May.

Getting there: Fly from Adelaide to Port Lincoln by small aircraft, then transfer to a live-aboard boat. Regulations protecting sea lions during the pupping season mean many boats operate around the Neptune Islands instead of Dangerous Reef.

Quality of Marine Life: Great White Sharks are the major attraction. The cages may be lowered to the bottom to see the sharks or other fish attracted by the chum. At quiet times divers may dive with Australian Sea Lions or go ashore to visit New Zealand Fur Seal colonies.

Dive Practicalities: Suitable for divers who have done at least 100 dives so that they are able to use

their diving equipment without having to think about it. For stability within the cages, divers are intentionally overweighted.

PACIFIC OCEAN

Thailand - Whale Sharks

Star Rating: ★

Location: Andaman Sea.

Climate: Dominated by monsoons. Heavy rains and strong winds from May–Oct. Year-round temperatures range from 21–34°C (70–93°F).

Water temperature: Averages 27–31°C (81–88°F).

Visibility: Best from Nov–Apr; ranges from 5–30m (16–100ft).

Depth: From 5m (16ft) on reefs to 50m+ (165ft+) and more on drop-offs.

Snorkelling: Yes.

Best time to go: Nov–Apr when visibility is good.

Getting there: Fly to Phuket via Bangkok.

Quality of Marine Life: Good with a variety of species, including sharks, corals and pelagic fish.

Dive practicalities: Currents can be strong.

Malaysia - Terumbu Layang-Layang, Sipadan and Sangalaki

Star Rating: ★ Turtles on Sipadan and Sangalaki, ★★ Hammerheads at Terumbu Layang-Layang, ★★ Turtle Cavern, Sipadan.

Location: Layang-Layang: Remote wall-diving site 300km (190 miles) northwest of Kota Kinabalu, Sabah, Borneo. Sipadan: Island resort 35km (22 miles) off Semporna on Sabah's east coast.

Climate: Tropical with two main seasons; warm and humid year-round. Terumbu's only resort is closed during the northeast monsoon (Nov–Feb). Sipadan not affected by monsoons. Temperatures range from 26–30°C (79–86°F).

Water temperature: 25–31°C (77–88°F).

Visibility: Both sites approach the mythical 60m (200ft), rarely drop below 30m (100ft).

Depth of Dives: Suitable for all standards of divers but the walls descend deeper than sport divers should dive. The large shoals of Hammerheads are often too deep for novices, but in such good visibility they can usually be seen from above.

Snorkelling: Excellent at both sites.

Best time to go: Best weather Apr–Sep. April and May are when large shoals of Hammerhead Sharks are often encountered at Layang-Layang. Sipadan can be crowded in peak holiday season (Aug).

Getting there: Layang-Layang: fly to Kota Kinabalu in Sabah, then short flight by small aircraft to Layang-Layang. Sipadan: by road from Kota Kinabalu to Semporna, then via resort speedboat.

Quality of Marine Life: Diverse and prolific, good corals, reef fish and pelagic species.

Dive Practicalities: The strong currents and upwellings which surge around the wall at Layang-Layang (the time when most Hammerhead Sharks and other pelagic species are encountered) can be minimized by careful use of the tide tables. Large

swells can occur during rough weather. Sipadan's caverns are not suitable for divers who suffer from claustrophobia. Good buoyancy, an underwater light and a backup light are essential.

Micronesia - Chuuk, Palau and Yap islands

Star Rating: ★ Blue Corner, Palau; ★ Manta Rays at Yap; ★ to ★★★ Truk Lagoon (Chuuk).

Location: Mid-Pacific islands, east of Philippines.

Climate: Tropical, with little seasonal variation. Temperatures range from 25–30°C (77–86°F). Dry season Jan–May. Typhoon season Aug–Dec.

Water Temperature: 28–30°C (82–86°F).

Visibility: Truk Lagoon: from 12m (40ft) at low tide to over 30m (100ft) at high, depending on tides and location within the lagoon. Can be more than 30m (100ft) at Yap and Palau.

Depth of Dives: Truk Lagoon: most diving is from 12–24m (40–80ft). Some deeper wrecks are at 30–46m (100–150ft). Yap depths around 15m (50ft), Palau from 30m (100ft).

Snorkelling: Snorkelling is possible on a number of Truk's wrecks, although most require scuba. Good snorkelling on the reefs at Palau.

Best Time to Go: Diving is good all year round, but water conditions are best from Jan–May.

Getting there: By air from Guam, Palau or Manila.

Quality of Marine Life: Schooling fish and invertebrate life. Soft and hard corals drape the wrecks.

Dive Practicalities: Conditions are normally calm at Truk Lagoon, with ample diving at all levels. Penetration of wrecks and deeper wrecks should be attempted only by experienced divers accompanied by a local guide. Visibility in the channels at Yap is best toward the end of a flood tide. At Palau, circumstances depend on the strength of the current and whether or not divers use reef hooks.

Philippines - Puerto Galera (canyons), Coron (wrecks)

Star Rating: ★★ to ★★★ for wrecks and canyons.

Location: Widespread island group between South China Sea and Pacific Ocean. Puerto Galera is a large island near Batangas, south of Manila. Coron and Busuanga islands lie south of Mindoro Island.

Climate: Tropical with distinct seasons due to the monsoons. Temperatures 23–36°C (73–97°F).

Water temperature: 25–31°C (77–88°F).

Visibility: Up to 30m (100ft) depending on the weather. Visibility in Gunter's Cavern depends on tides and the prowess of other divers.

Depth of Dives: Coron wrecks: From 12–42m (40–138ft). Gunter's Cavern: maximum depth 14m (44ft). Canyons at Puerto Galera: up to 60m (200ft), deeper than sport divers should dive.

Snorkelling: Good on the shallow wrecks and nearby reefs at Coron and Puerto Galera.

Best time to go: Best months Mar–Oct. Busuanga-Coron area can be dived all year round but the airstrip may be closed temporarily by heavy rain. Jan–Jul avoids the possibility of typhoons.

Getting there: Puerto Galera: fly to Manila, then travel by road to Batangas and transfer to bancas (boats with outrigger stabilizers) for Sabang Beach. Due to their outriggers, bancas are not capable of mooring side-on to a jetty, and passengers may have to wade ashore at Sabang Beach, so wear shorts and sandals. Larger public ferries go from Batangas to Puerto Galera's Poblaçion pier from where divers can hire a banca to Sabang Beach. Coron: from Manila via small aircraft to Busuanga Island (limited baggage) or air conditioned ferry (14 hours, no baggage limit). Accommodation, dive operators and live-aboard boats can be found in Coron town on Busuanga Island.

Quality of Marine Life: Diverse and prolific, with a wide variety of marine species, including larger pelagic fish on the offshore reefs.

Dive Practicalities: Puerto Galera: it is easy to lose concentration, so divers should watch their air consumption and depth and try to stay together. The current often flows too fast to use a surface marker buoy (SMB) for the deeper parts of the dive so divers should carry a delayed deployment surface marker buoy for use at the end of the dive. Gunter's Cavern: only for cool-headed divers who do not suffer from claustrophobia. Underwater lights are useful, but not when the sediment has been disturbed.
Coron wrecks: suitable for all divers, except for deep dives and lengthwise penetration, which are only for more advanced divers. An underwater light and backup light are necessary for penetration.

Vanuatu - *President Coolidge*
Star Rating: ★ to ★★★
Location: Pacific island group east of Australia.
Climate: Two seasons: summer (Nov–Mar), winter (Apr–Oct). Temperatures range from 23–28°C (73–82°F).
Water temperature: 25–30°C (77–86°F).
Visibility: Generally 15–20m (50–65ft) on the wreck but can be as much as 30m (100ft).
Depth of Dives: 15–70m (50–230ft), be careful of the maximum depth.
Snorkelling: Only for excellent snorkellers.
Best time to go: Year round.
Getting there: Fly from Sydney or Auckland to Port Villa on Efate and connect to Espiritu Santo.
Quality of Marine Life: Good, most Pacific species can be found.
Dive Practicalities: Easier sections of the *President Coolidge* are suitable for all levels of diver, but penetration lengthwise and deep dives to the stern are only for very experienced and competent divers who have a thorough understanding of decompression. Extra cylinders of air or Nitrox fitted with regulators should be hung at suitable decompression stop depths. For penetration, if you are not with a guide, tie a safety guideline from outside. Carry a powerful underwater light and backup light. Dives deeper than 50m (165ft) are beyond depths recommended for diving on air by most training agencies.

Great Barrier Reef - *Yongala*
Star Rating: ★★
Location: Between the Great Barrier Reef and the Queensland coast. Nearest towns: Bowen and Townsville.
Climate: Tropical, temperatures from 24–28°C (75–82°F) but cooler at sea especially when the wind is blowing. Cyclone season is officially Jan–Mar but December is also usually rough.
Water temperature: 22–27°C (72–81°F).
Visibility: Generally poor, it can be up to 30m (100ft) but may be as low as 5m (16ft).
Depth of Dives: Maximum 30m (100ft) but can be restricted to 22m (72ft).
Snorkelling: Possible in calm weather.
Best time to go: Avoid potential cyclone months.
Getting there: Fly to Townsville. *Yongala* is a live-aboard-only destination taken as a 2–3 day excursion from Townsville or as part of a longer cruise.
Quality of Marine Life: Exceptional, abundant and the fish are unusually large.
Dive Practicalities: With no protection from the wind, there will often be occasions when the wreck cannot be dived. Although suitable for all levels of diver, when the currents are strong the wreck is best dived by strong, experienced swimmers. Good chase-boat cover is essential. No extra equipment required but an underwater light is useful and divers should carry an SMB or rescue tube.

French Polynesia (Tahiti) - Sharks
Star Rating: ★
Location: Pacific island group.
Climate: Tropical. Warm and humid Nov–Apr, dry season May–Oct. Average temperature 25°C (77°F).
Water temperature: 23–28°C (73–82°F).
Visibility: 18–46m (60–150ft).
Depth: From 15–23m (50–75ft) at Moorea, variable at other dive sites.
Snorkelling: Scuba only for shark dives, snorkelling is possible at other sites.
Best time to go: Conditions good year round, but best diving is in the dry season.
Getting there: Fly to Papeete, then local flights or ferry to other islands.
Quality of Marine Life: Many Indo-Pacific species, including marine mammals. Healthy coral growth.
Dive practicalities: Some experience and good buoyancy control required for shark dives.

Cocos and Malpelo Islands - Hammerhead Sharks
Star Rating: ★★★ Cocos, ★★★★ Malpelo.
Location: Pacific islands off the coast of Costa Rica (Cocos Island) and Colombia (Malpelo Island).
Climate: Tropical with two seasons, average rainfall 2540mm (100in) at Cocos and 1060mm (42in) at Malpelo. Temperatures reach 32°C (90°F) on the coast but are lower at sea. The dry season provides calmer seas for the long boat journey to the islands, but most Hammerhead Sharks are encountered during the rainy season.

Water temperature: 25–28°C (77–82°F).
Visibility: 9–24m (30–80ft) in the wet season, 20–30m (65–100ft) in the dry season.
Depth of Dives: Cocos Island 18–40m (60–130ft); Malpelo, from surface to 40m (surface to 130ft).
Snorkelling: Take care near to bait-balls.
Best time to go: Dry season: Nov–May, wet season: Jun–Nov. Jul–Aug for Hammerhead Sharks.
Getting there: Fly to San Jose, Costa Rica. Transfer by road to Puntarenus to meet live-aboard boats for Cocos; fly on to Golfito for Malpelo.
Quality of Marine Life: Larger animals are prolific, there is no coral so fish are the major attraction.
Dive Practicalities: Suitable only for advanced divers. Ear infections are common so carry and use a suitable proprietary ear-drying agent to avoid them. Non-photographers will find gloves useful for holding on to rocks in the current and surge.

Southern California - Shark dives
Star Rating: ★
Location: Open ocean dives take place up to 40km (25 miles) offshore between mainland and Catalina Island; further out for San Clemente Island.
Climate: Mediterranean, dry summers Apr–Nov, Nov–Mar can have rain. Temperatures 15–26°C (60–80°F) in summer, 10–20°C (50–68°F) in winter.
Water temperature: 13°C (55°F) in winter, 21°C (70°F) in summer.
Visibility: Can be affected by chum in the water.
Depth: 6–9m (20–30ft).
Snorkelling: May be allowed on some shark dives.
Best time to go: Year round. Best times Aug–Nov.
Getting there: Fly to Los Angeles or San Diego.
Quality of Marine Life: On open ocean dives little marine life except sharks, sea lions, *Mola molas*.
Dive practicalities: Good buoyancy skills are essential for cage diving.

CARIBBEAN & ATLANTIC OCEAN

British Virgin Islands - RMS *Rhone*
Star Rating: ★
Location: Caribbean island group, located some 95km (60 miles) east of Puerto Rico.
Climate: Sub-tropical, temperatures 25–30°C (77–86°F) but trade winds have a moderating effect on the climate. Hurricanes possible Aug–Oct.
Water temperature: 25–28°C (77–82°F).
Visibility: Generally over 30m (100ft).
Depth of Dives: 24m (79ft) on the RMS *Rhone*.
Snorkelling: Good over the shallow section of the wreck and over the reef behind.
Best time to go: Avoid hurricane months though there will often be cheap deals at this time.
Getting there: Direct flights from Europe to Tortola (BVI) and from America to St. Thomas (USVI). Connecting flights from other Caribbean islands, including many through San Juan (Puerto Rico), may be in small aircraft with baggage limits.
Quality of Marine Life: Good, most Caribbean species can be found.

Dive Practicalities: Suitable for all divers so long as the currents are not too strong. Penetration is easy and safe. No extra equipment required but an underwater light is useful for bringing out colours.

Bahamas – Dolphins, shark feeds and Blue Holes

Star Rating: ★ Dolphins and shark feeds.
★ to ★★★ Blue holes.

Location: Group of more than 3000 islands and cays scattered across 160,000km² (100,000 square miles) of ocean, 74 km (46 miles) from Florida.

Climate: Mild tropical, temperatures range from 24–29°C (75–84°F).

Water temperature: Variable, 22–29°C (72–84°F) across several thermoclines.

Visibility: 1.5–9m (5–30ft) at the surface, clear below 27m (90ft).

Depth of Dives: Variable, from 3–9m (10–30ft) to view the dolphins at White Sand Ridge, to over 50m (165ft) in some of the blue holes and caves.

Snorkelling: Preferred at dolphin dives, and good at some blue holes where the surface water has reasonable visibility.

Best time to go: Year round. Hurricanes are rare but possible from Jul–Oct.

Getting there: Daily international flights, many via Miami and other US hubs, to Nassau and Freeport, then via inter-island connections.

Quality of Marine Life: Diverse and unique.

Dive Practicalities: The training necessary for diving the blue holes is available from local operators who also provide a guide, both for safety and for protection of the fragile ecosystem. Many inland blue holes require a short walk where mosquitoes and other biting insects can be a nuisance. Marine blue holes can have strong currents.

Grand Cayman Island – Stingray City

Star Rating: ★

Location: Central Caribbean, south of Cuba and 290km (175 miles) west-northwest of Jamaica.

Climate: Fine weather year-round. Temperatures average 30–40°C (86–104°F) in summer, dropping to around 20°C (70°F) for a short winter period.

Water temperature: 27–28°C (80–82°F).

Visibility: The deep oceanic Cayman Trench contributes to the clarity of the water and provides spectacular wall dives.

Depth: As shallow as 1m (3ft) at The Sandbar to deep dives over the Cayman Trench drop-offs.

Snorkelling: Yes.

Best time to go: Best months are May–Sep but the islands are good for year-round diving.

Getting there: Direct flights from Europe or via Miami from the USA. Regular connections between the three islands in the group.

Quality of Marine Life: Stingrays are a major attraction but reefs, wrecks and walls offer a variety of corals, fish and other marine life.

Dive practicalities: Most diving and snorkelling is from day boats, with a short ride to the dive sites.

Mexico – Cozumel (currents) and Yucatán (cenotes)

Star Rating: ★ to ★★★★★

Location: Yucatán Peninsula and Cozumel Island face into the Gulf of Mexico and the Caribbean.

Climate: Generally pleasant and tropical all year round, humid Sep–Jan. Average temperature 20°C (68°F) in winter, up to 40°C (104°F) in summer. Hurricane season Aug–Dec.

Water temperature: From 22–24°C (72–75°F) in winter and early spring to 24–29°C (75–84°F) in summer and fall. Cenotes usually 24°C (75°F) except after rain or in those connected to the sea.

Visibility: Close to the mythical 60m (200ft) in cenotes when clear, but lower after rain. Visibility at sea ranges from 24–38m (80–125ft).

Depth of Dives: Most popular cenote dives are from the surface to 12m (40ft). Sea dives mostly 10–34m (30–110ft).

Snorkelling: Some cenotes have snorkelling facilities for day trippers. Snorkelling generally good all around Cozumel Island.

Best time to go: Nov–Mar for clear water in the Cenotes; Apr–Aug for other dives.

Getting there: Fly to Cancún from Mexico City or from various hubs in the USA.

Quality of Marine Life: A variety of freshwater tropical fish in the cenotes, including the Yucatán Tetra and High-fin Mollies. Where a cenote is connected to the sea, there will be a mixture of freshwater and saltwater organisms. Healthy coral reefs with tropical Caribbean species.

Dive Practicalities: Ample opportunities for divers of all levels. Those wishing to participate in deeper dives and drift dives need good buoyancy skills, and a dive guide is recommended for diving in the strong currents. Divers not trained in cavern or cave diving are advised to take a guided tour of the cenotes, for which an underwater light and backup light should be carried. The fish may be small but they tend to nibble at exposed flesh so a full wet suit or old clothing is useful as protection. Although many of the cenotes are suitable for all levels of diver, the more complicated explorations require full cave diving techniques and the highest levels of diving proficiency.

US East Coast – Wrecks

Star Rating: ★ to ★★★★

Location: *Duane* and *Bibb*, Florida Keys; *Proteus*, off Cape Hatteras, North Carolina; *Andrea Doria*, off Nantucket, Massachusetts.

Climate: The Florida Keys are subtropical, with temperatures from 18–23°C (65–73°F) in winter, up to 30°C (86°F) in summer and autumn (fall). Hurricane season in the Keys and along the North Carolina coast is from Aug–Dec. The northeastern USA has a temperate climate with temperatures below freezing possible from Nov–Apr.

Water Temperature: In the Keys, temperatures average 22–29°C (72–84°F) in late summer and fall; off North Carolina, the range is from 13°C (55°F) in winter and spring to 24–26°C (75–79°F) in late summer and fall; for the northeast, water temperatures range from 7°C (45°F) in winter and spring to 15°C (60°F) in late summer and autumn (fall).

Visibility: Visibility in the Keys ranges from 18–38m (60–125ft); North Carolina and the northeast coast wrecks can have visibility from less than 1m (3ft) to well over 30m (100ft).

Depth of Dives: The *Duane* and *Bibb* are at 28m (90ft) and 40m (130ft) respectively. Most of the popular North Carolina wrecks are in the 24–46m (80–150ft) range. Northeast wrecks range from shallow to quite deep, with some popular technical dive sites exceeding 60m (200ft).

Snorkelling: No snorkelling.

Best Time to Go: In the Florida Keys, diving is good all year round, but is best from May–Aug. For the northeast coast and off North Carolina, diving is best from Jun–Oct.

Getting There: The Florida Keys are reached via Miami; the North Carolina wrecks are accessible from a number of cities, including Morehead City, Beaufort, Wilmington and Hatteras; northeast wreck diving takes place out of various towns and cities, including Atlantic City, New Jersey; Long Beach, New York; New Bedford, Massachusetts.

Quality of Marine Life: The Florida Keys have a rich collection of tropical species, with many large fish such as groupers and barracuda; North Carolina wrecks have both cold water and tropical species, which ride the Gulf Stream up from the south. Especially interesting in North Carolina waters are large numbers of Sand Tiger Sharks that congregate in the fall; northeast wrecks have cold water species, including lobsters.

Dive Practicalities: The *Duane* and *Bibb*, in the Florida Keys, can be enjoyed by most divers, subject to depth comfort and experience; North Carolina wrecks are more accessible and can be enjoyed by reasonably experienced divers; many of the northeast wrecks, including the *Andrea Doria*, are for experienced technical divers only.

CONVERSION CHART		
FROM	TO	MULTIPLY BY
Centimetres	inches	0.394
Inches	centimetres	2.54
Metres	feet	3.28
Feet	metres	0.305
Metres	yards	1.09
Yards	metres	0.914
Kilometres	miles	0.621
Miles	kilometres	1.61
Kilograms	pounds	2.20
Pounds	kilograms	0.454

To convert Celsius to Fahrenheit:
  (1.8 x degrees Celsuis) +32.
To convert Fahrenheit to Celsius:
  (Degrees Fahrenheit -32) x 0.5555.

INDEX

PUBLISHER'S ACKNOWLEDGEMENTS

The publishers would like to thank the following text contributors: **Chris Fallows** Great White Sharks, Western Cape; **Andy Cobb** Raggedtooth sharks, Aliwal Shoal and Protea Banks; **Danja Köhler** Jellyfish Lake, Palau and Kakaban, Two Oceans Aquarium; **Anne Storrie** Whale sharks, sea snakes, Ningaloo Reef and Underwater World; **Martyn Farr** Wookey Hole; **Jim Mastro** Antarctica. In addition, sincere thanks are due to the two main contributors, **Jack Jackson** and **Al Hornsby**, for their invaluable assistance and advice at all stages of the project, from initial conception through to final proofs.

PHOTOGRAPHIC ACKNOWLEDGEMENTS

Copyright in photography is held by the following photographers and/or their agents:

Front cover: Ken Hoppen (Legend Photography); *back cover* (clockwise from top left): Gavin Newman, Altus Pienaar, Peter Pinnock, Art Womack (Tom Campbell), Lawson Wood, Kelvin Aitken; *spine:* Geoff Spiby; *back flap:* Abdullah Rafiq.

Kelvin Aitken pp. 74–75; **Michael Aw** pp. 8-9, 11 (top), 56, 66 (top), 77 (top left), 82, 84, 85 (top), 86, 91 (top), 92 (left and right), 93 (top, bottom left and right),103 (bottom right), 104, 113 (top left), 116 (top), 117 (bottom right), 132 (top and bottom), 133 (right), 137 (top left), 144 (top); **Andy Belcher (Legend Photography)** pp. 124, 127; **Al Bruton** pp. 2–3 (title), 100–101; **Kevin Davidson (Graeme Teague Photography)** p. 107 (bottom); **Kevin Deacon** p. 29 (bottom); **Chris Fallows** p. 22 (centre and bottom); **Martyn Farr** pp. 11 (bottom), 139 (bottom), 149 (top); **Stephen Frink (Waterhouse)** pp. 128 (centre and bottom), 129 (top and bottom); **Gary Gentile** pp. 128 (top), 131 (bottom); **Itamar Grinberg** pp. 87, 89 (top right); **Kevin Gurr** p. 131 (top); **Al Hornsby** pp. 4–5 (imprint), 10 (bottom left), 14–15, 18 (bottom), 21 (left and right), 35 (top), 45 (top), 48, 49 (bottom), 50 (bottom), 53 (bottom), 54 (right and left), 55, 66 (top), 67, 80 (bottom), 83 (left, right top and centre), 88, 89 (bottom left), 97 (bottom), 103 (left), 105 (top and bottom), 106 (top and bottom), 108 (top and bottom), 109, 116 (bottom left), 117 (top and bottom left), 144 (bottom), 146 (top and bottom); **Paul Humann (Graeme Teague Photography)** pp. endpages, 17 (top), 37 (top and bottom), 38; **Jack Jackson** pp. 31 (bottom), 32 (top right and bottom), 33 (top right), 78, 79 (top left, centre and right, bottom), 90 (bottom), 91 (bottom left), 103 (top right), 113 (top right), 118 (top and bottom), 119 (top and bottom), 120, 121 (top left and right, bottom), 142, 143; **Tony Karacsonyi Photography** p. 125 (top and bottom); **Dennis King** p. 40 (top and bottom); **Danja Köhler** pp. 30, 45 (bottom), 57 (top left), 77 (top right), 83 bottom,91 (bottom right), 94 (top and bottom), 95 (left and right), 102; **Stefania Lamberti** pp. 41 (top), 42, 44 (top), 65 (bottom right); **Leopard Enterprises (Patrick Wagner)** pp.17 (centre), 23 (top and bottom), 25 (top left and right), 35 (bottom); **John Liddiard** pp. 21 (centre), 39 (top), 107 (top), 123 (right); **Lifefile (Sally-Anne Fison)** p. 80 (top); **Lochman Transparencies (Eva Boogaard)** pp. 17 (bottom right), 33 (bottom); **Lochman Transparencies (Geoff Taylor)** pp. 60–61, 62, 65 (bottom centre), 68–69, 85 (bottom), 90 (top); **Lochman Transparencies (Peter and Margie Nicholas)** p. 96 (top); **Lochman Transparencies (Alex Steffe)** pp. 12, 96 (bottom), 97 (top); **Jim Mastro** pp. 137 (bottom right), 150 (top and bottom), 151 (top left and right), 153 (left, right top and bottom); **Jim Mastro and Kristen Larson** p 152; **Naturescapes (Ann Storrie)** pp. 59 (top, centre and bottom), 99; **Naturescapes (C. Wayne Storrie)** p. 98; **Gavin Newman** pp 1, 13, 134–135, 136, 137 (top right), 138, 139 (top), 140 (right), 141 (top and bottom), 145 (top and bottom), 147 (top and bottom), 148 (top and bottom),149 (bottom); **Steven N. Norvich** p. 116 (bottom centre); **Altus Pienaar** p. 112 (right); **Peter Pinnock** pp. 41 (bottom), 43 (top), 43 (bottom), 44 (bottom), 110–111; **Brian Pitkin** pp. 70 (top), 71; **Linda Pitkin** pp. 31 (top), 122; **Bradley Sheard** p. 130 (top, bottom left and right); **Edward A.M. Snijders** pp. 112 (left), 113 (bottom right), 123 (left); **Geoff Spiby** pp. 22 (top), 24 (top and bottom), 25 (bottom), 26, 28 (left and right), 29 (top left and right), 32 (top left), 34, 57 (top right and bottom), 76; **Mark Strickland** pp. 63 (centre and bottom), 64, 65 (top and bottom left); **Graeme Teague** pp. 46 (top), 47, 50 (top), 52 (bottom); **Planet Earth Pictures (Kurt Amsler)** pp. 77 (bottom right); **Planet Earth Pictures (Darryl Torckler)** pp. 52–53 (top); **Twilight Zone (Becca Saunders)** pp. 18 (top), 19; **Twilight Zone (Mark Spencer)** pp. 20, 49 (top), 116 (bottom right), 126 (top and bottom); **Art Womack** pp. 10 (top left), 39 (top), 46 (bottom); **Art Womack (Barry Bosco)** p. 133 (left); **Art Womack (Tom Campbell)** pp. 16, 63 (top), 70 (bottom), 73, 81 (top); **Lawson Wood** pp 7, 51, 58, 81 (bottom), 89 (bottom right), 114, 115 (top and bottom), 140 (left).